MW00933561

Adult Coloring Book

50 Mandalas for Stress-Relief

Volume 1

By Zeny Creative

ISBN : 9781077810235

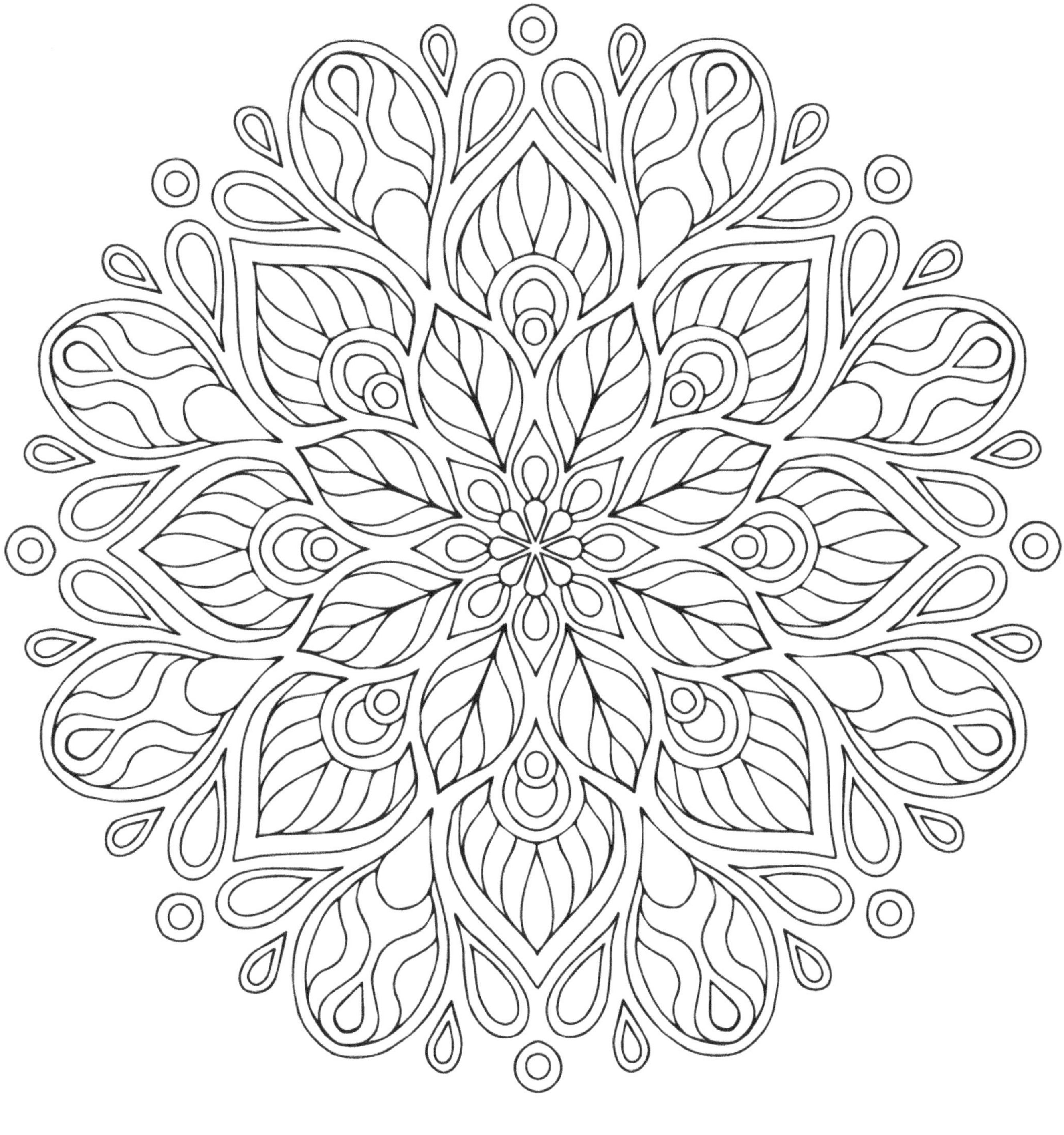

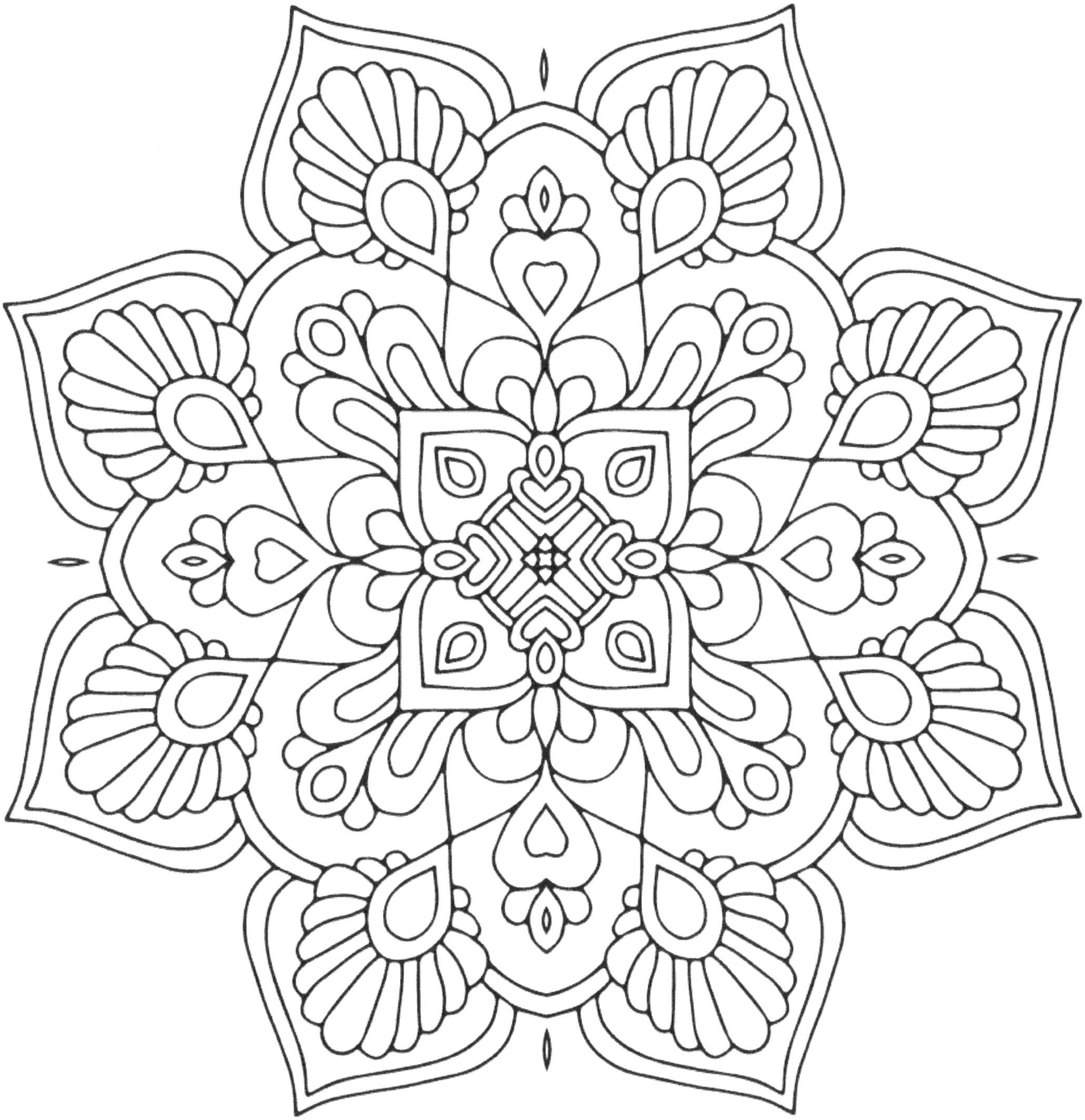

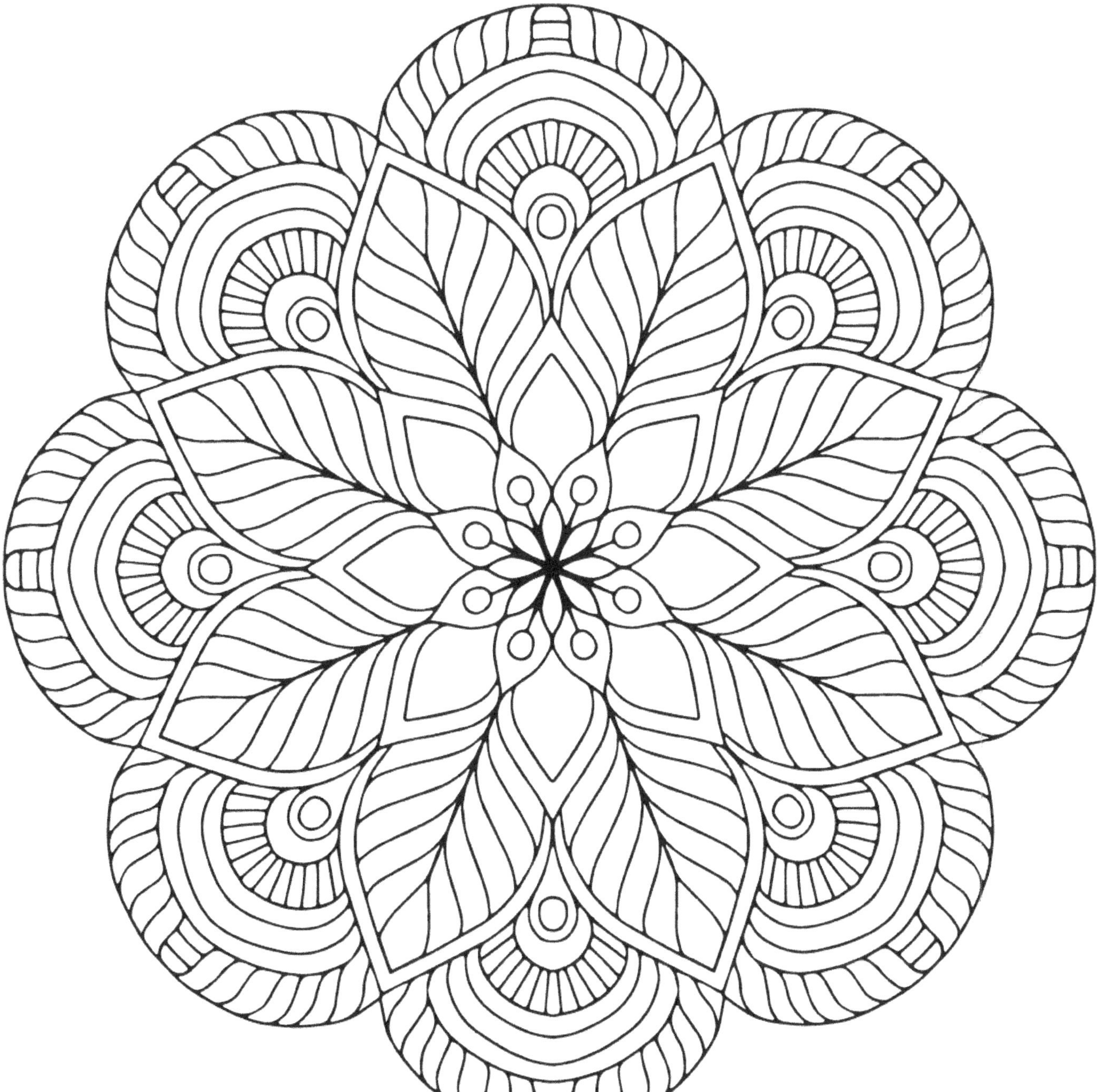

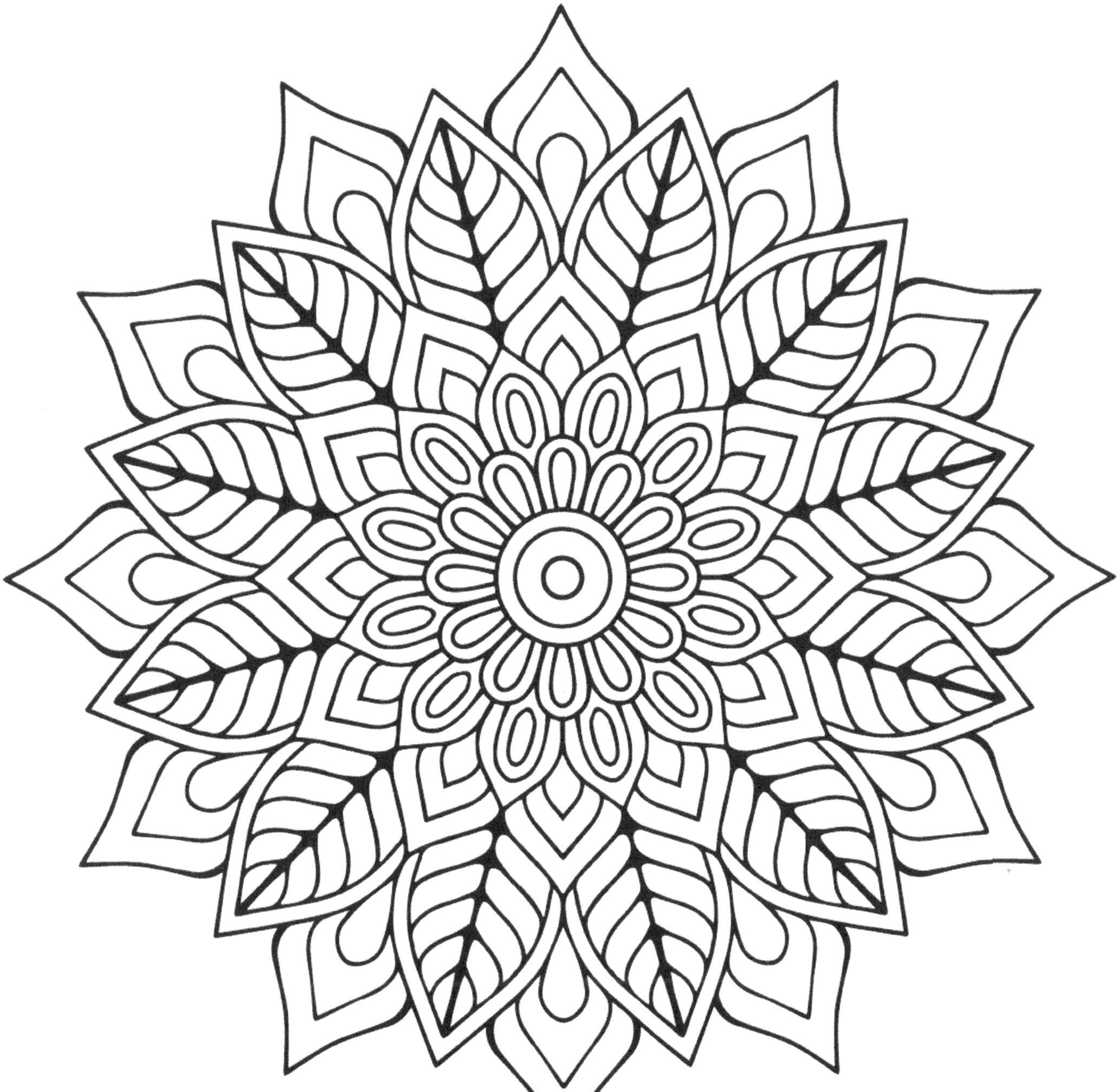

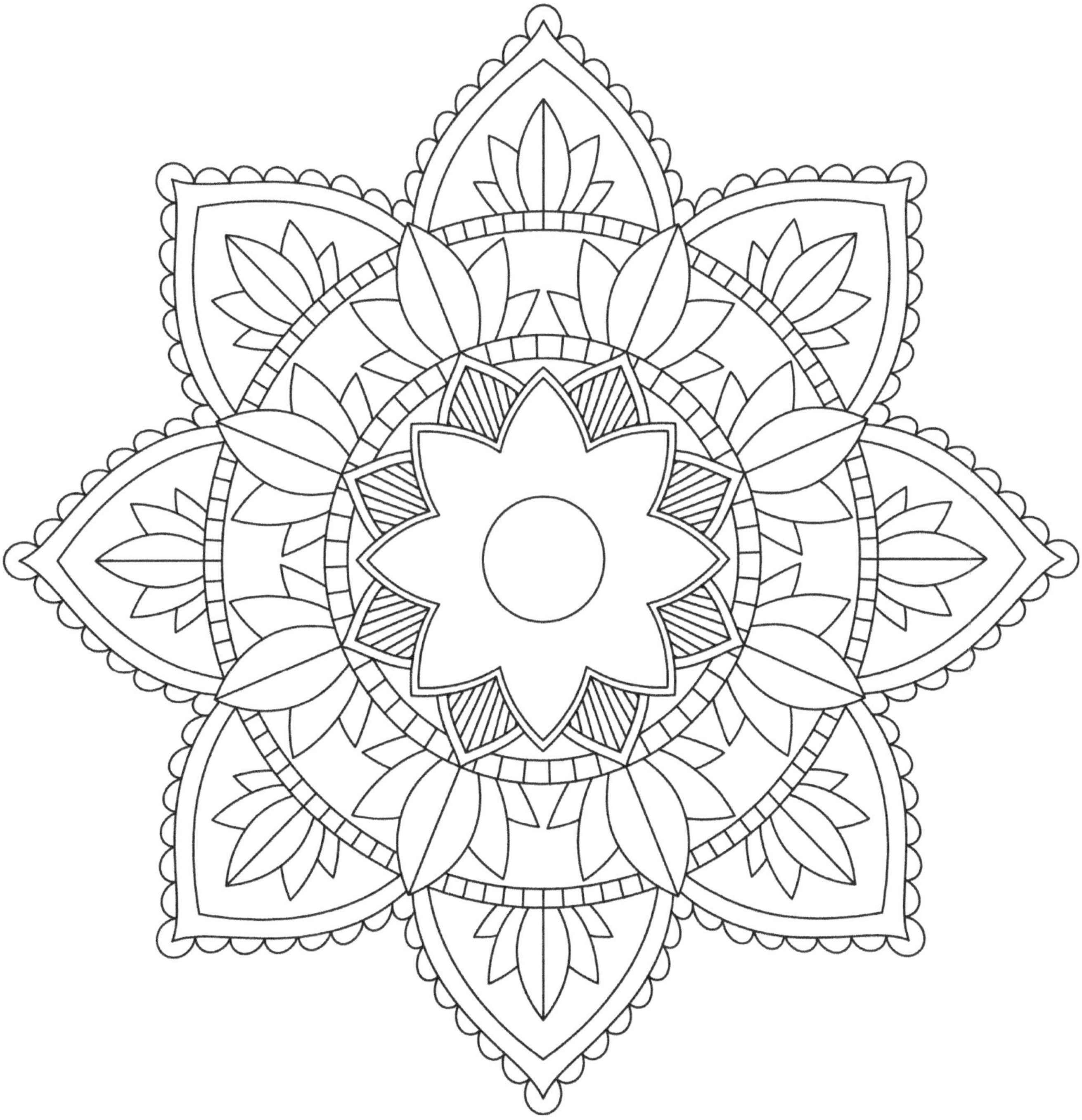

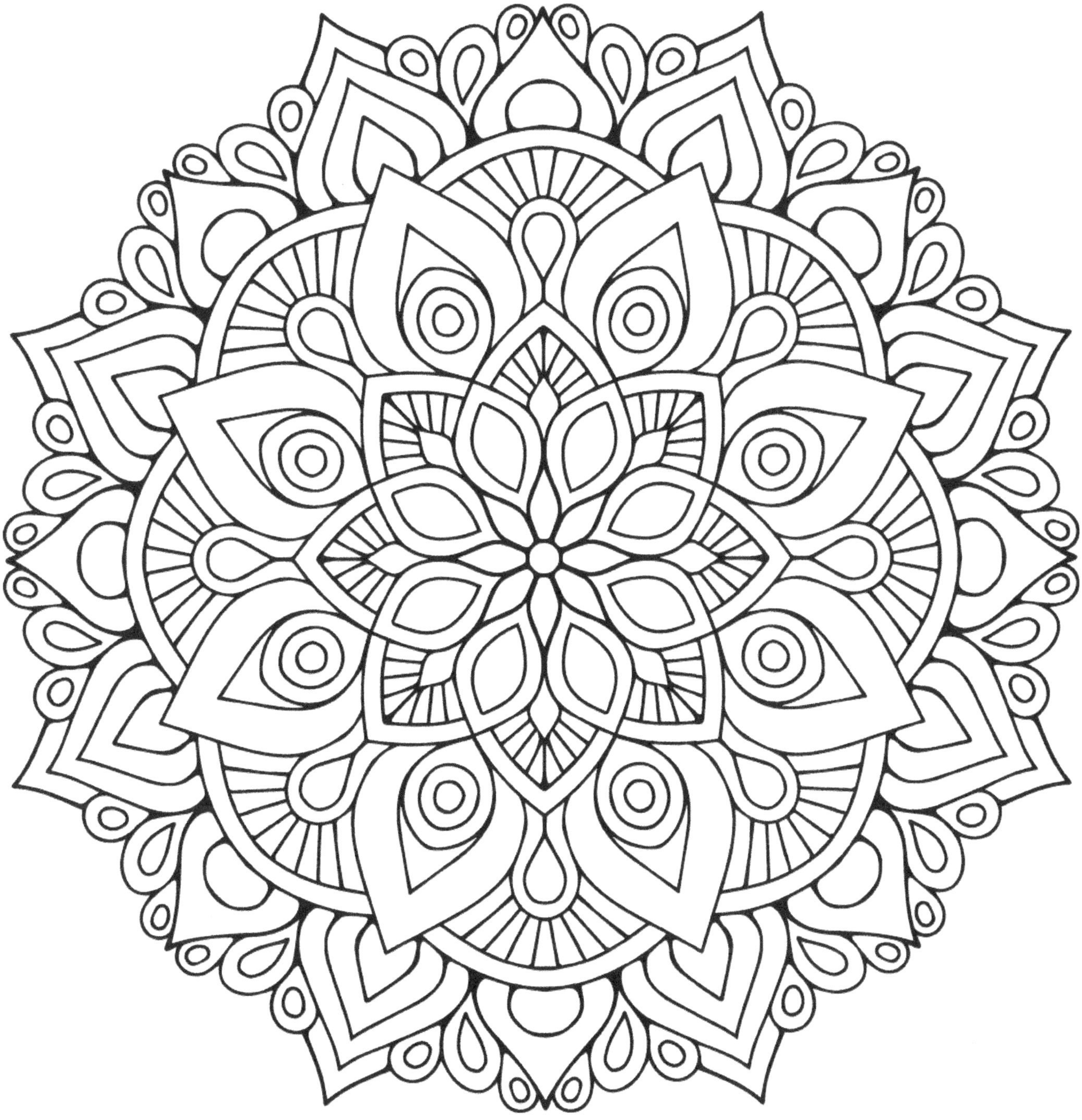

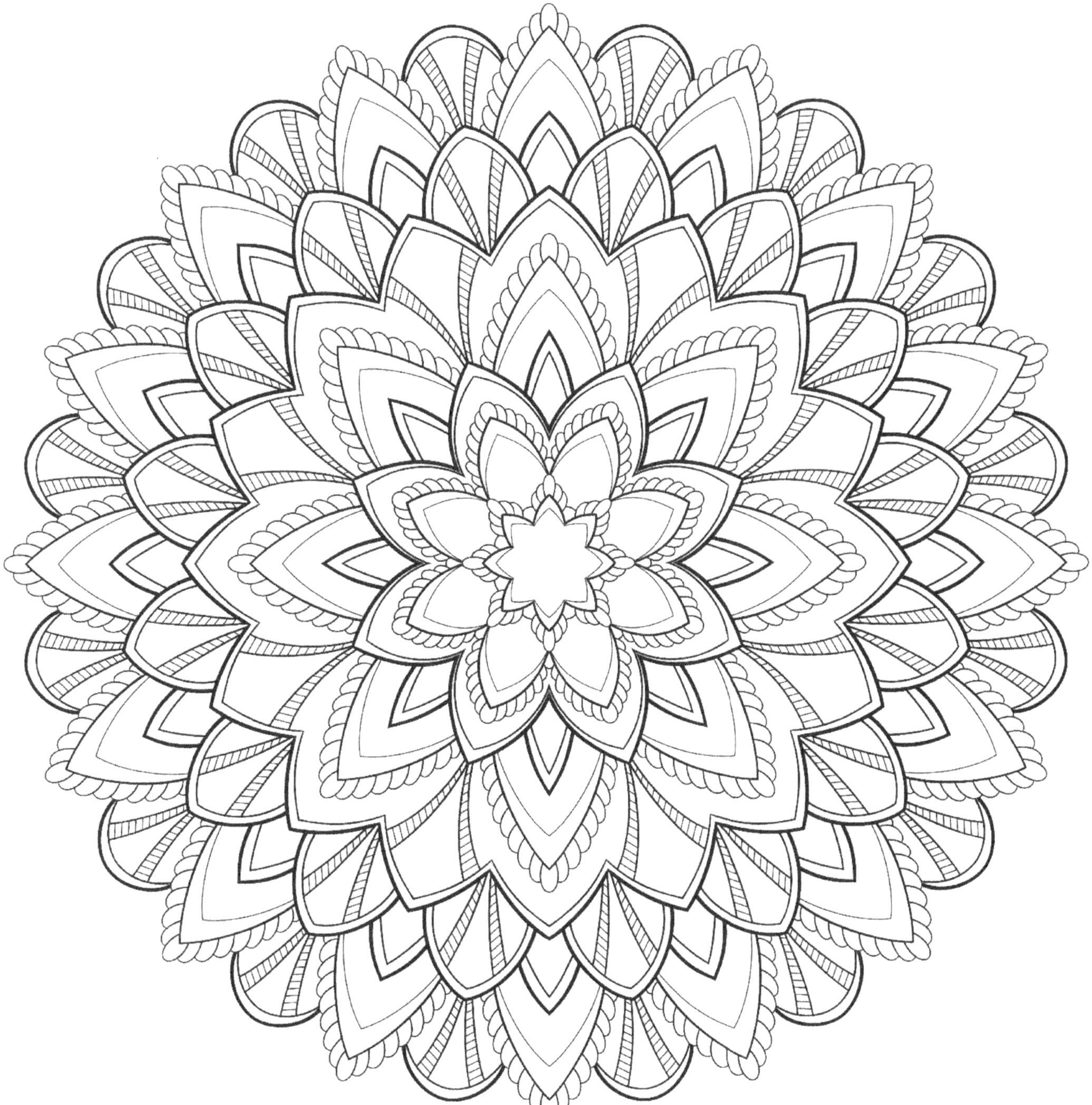

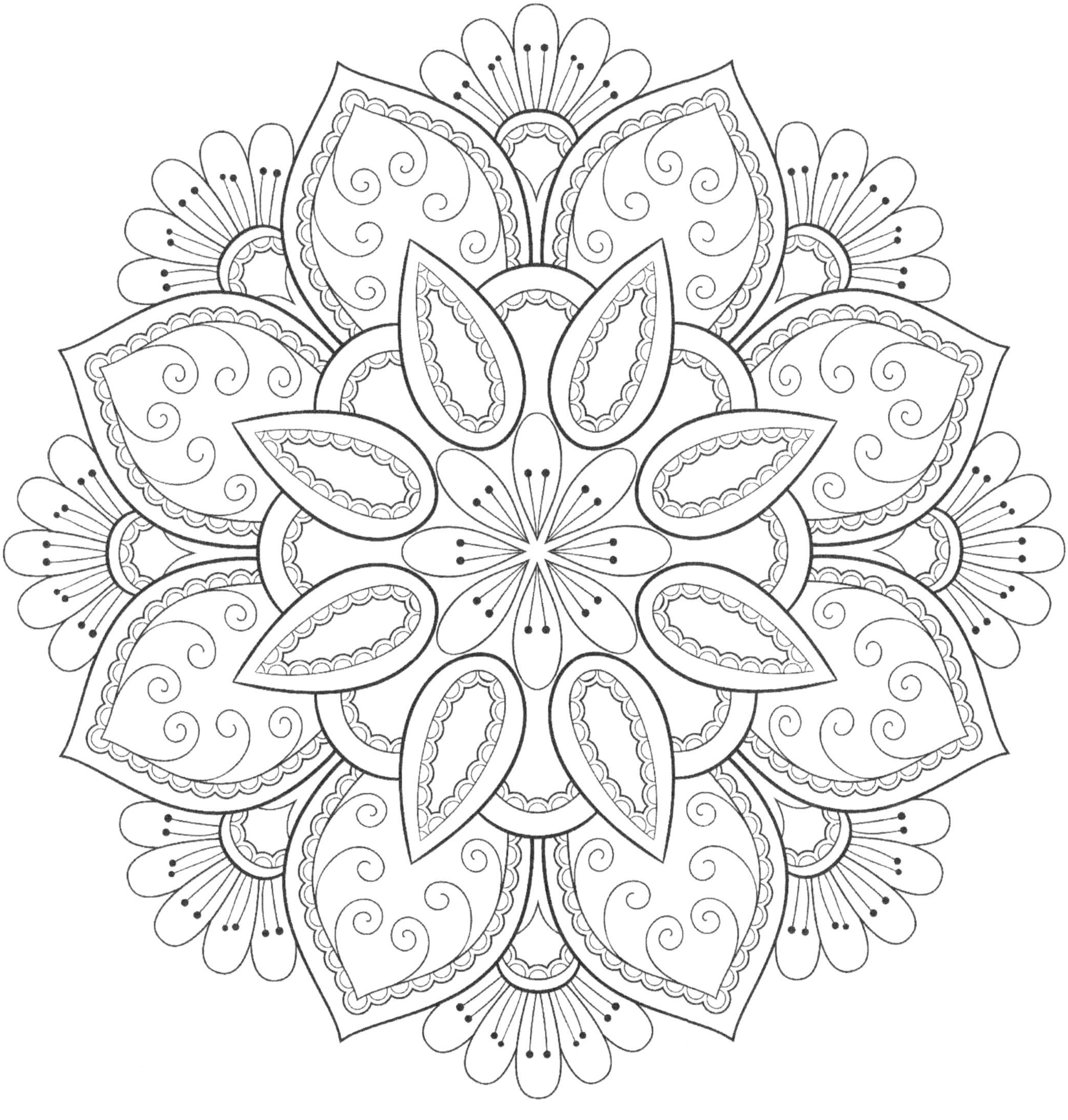

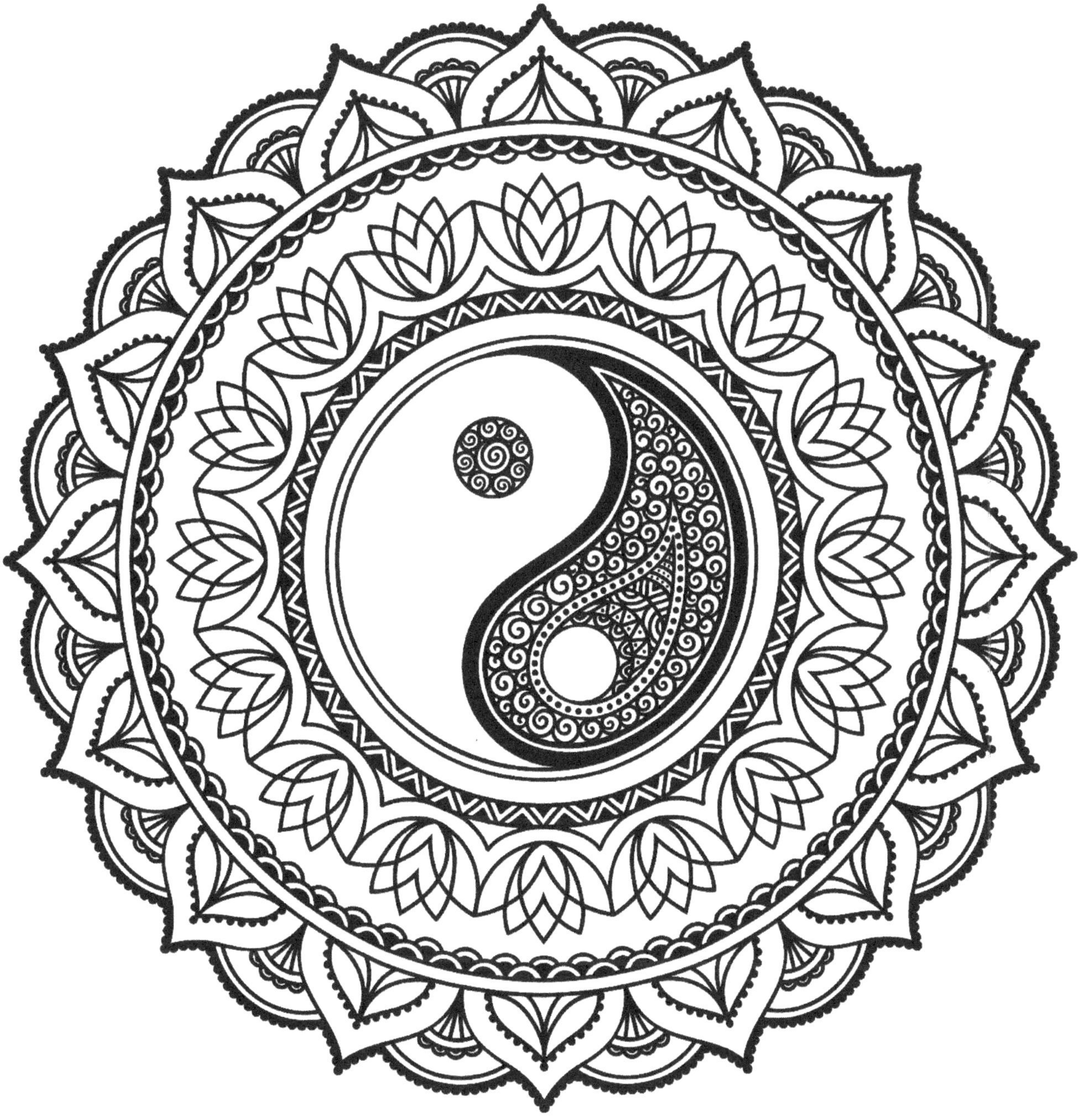

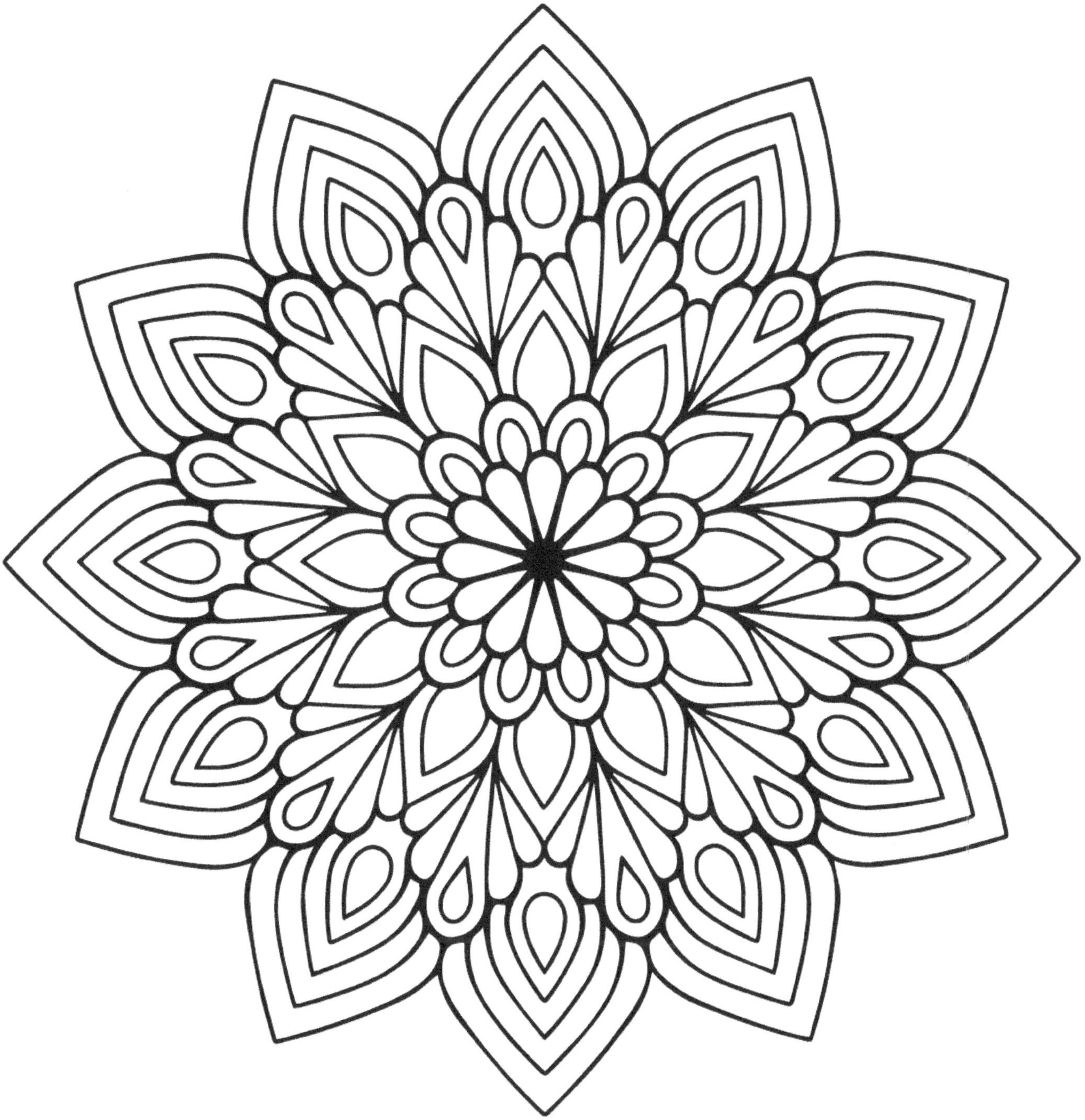

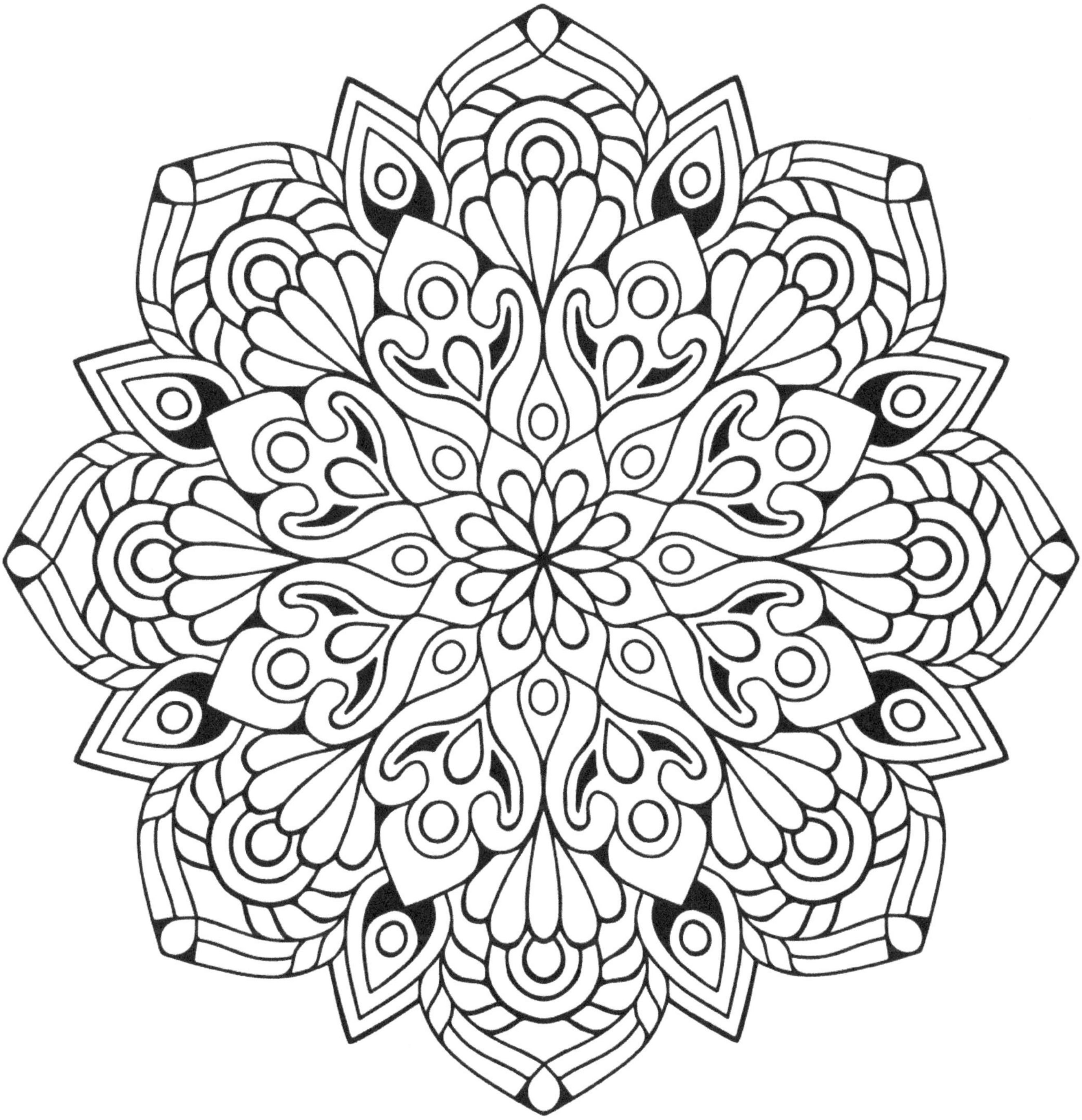

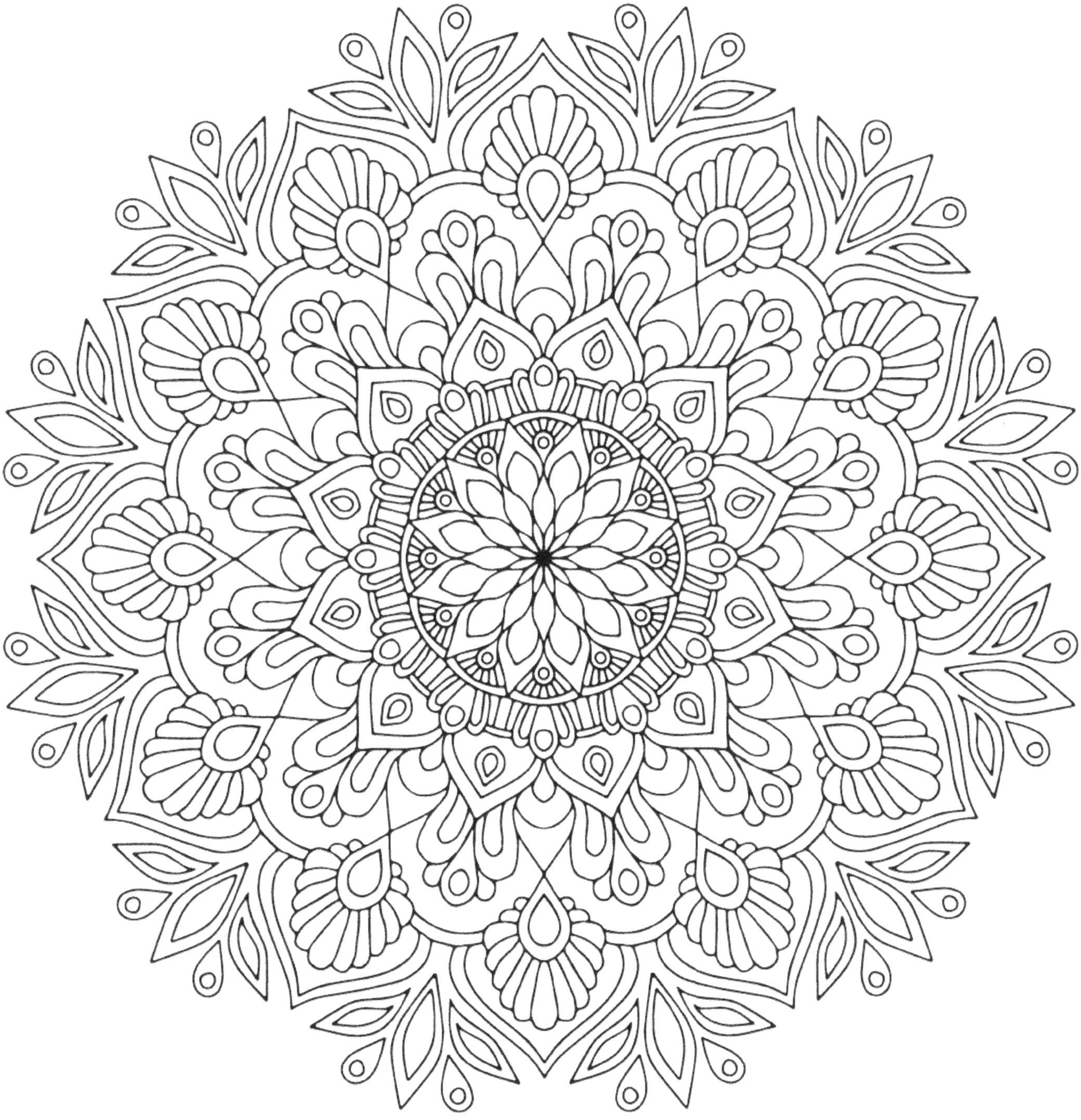

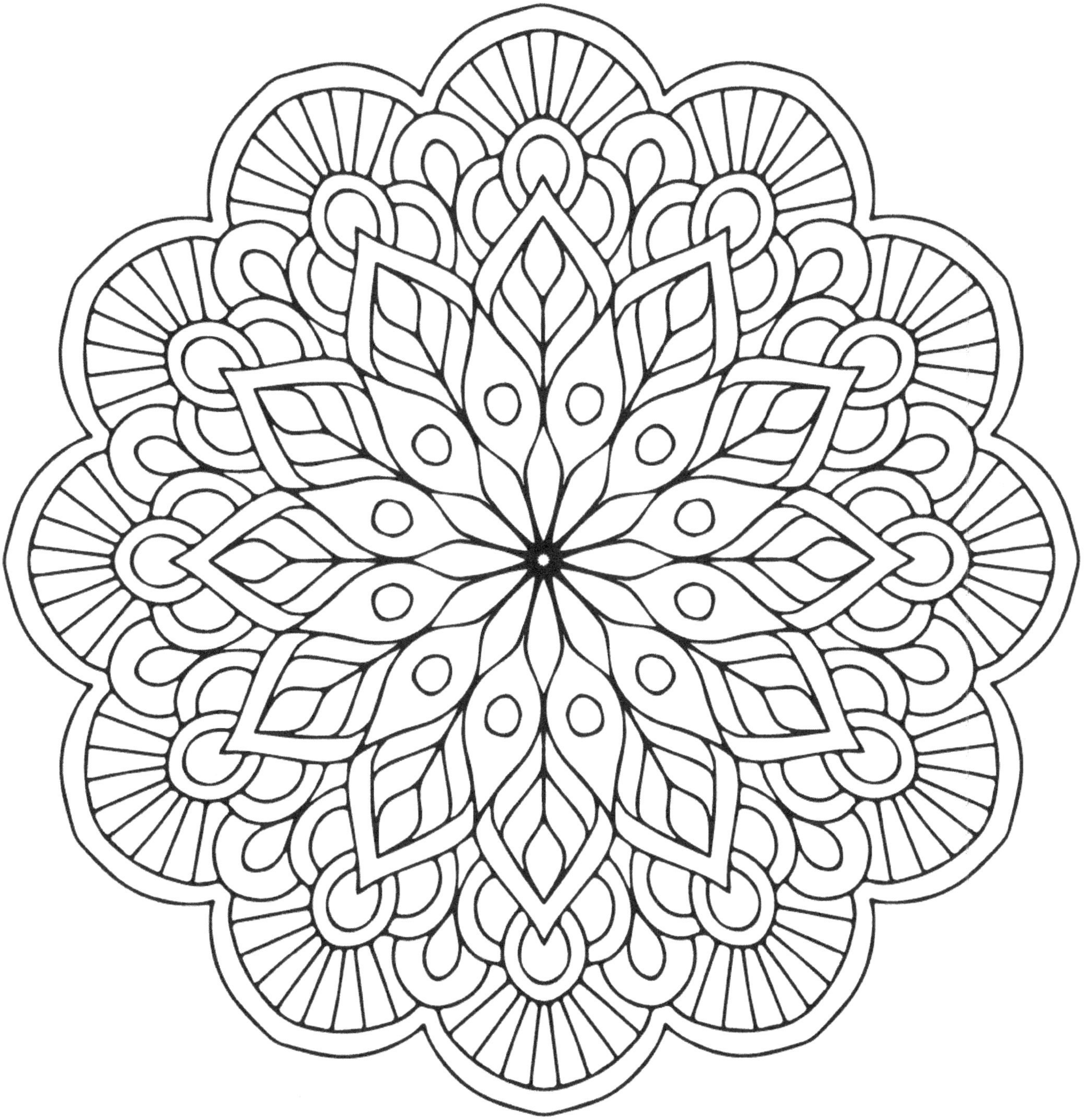

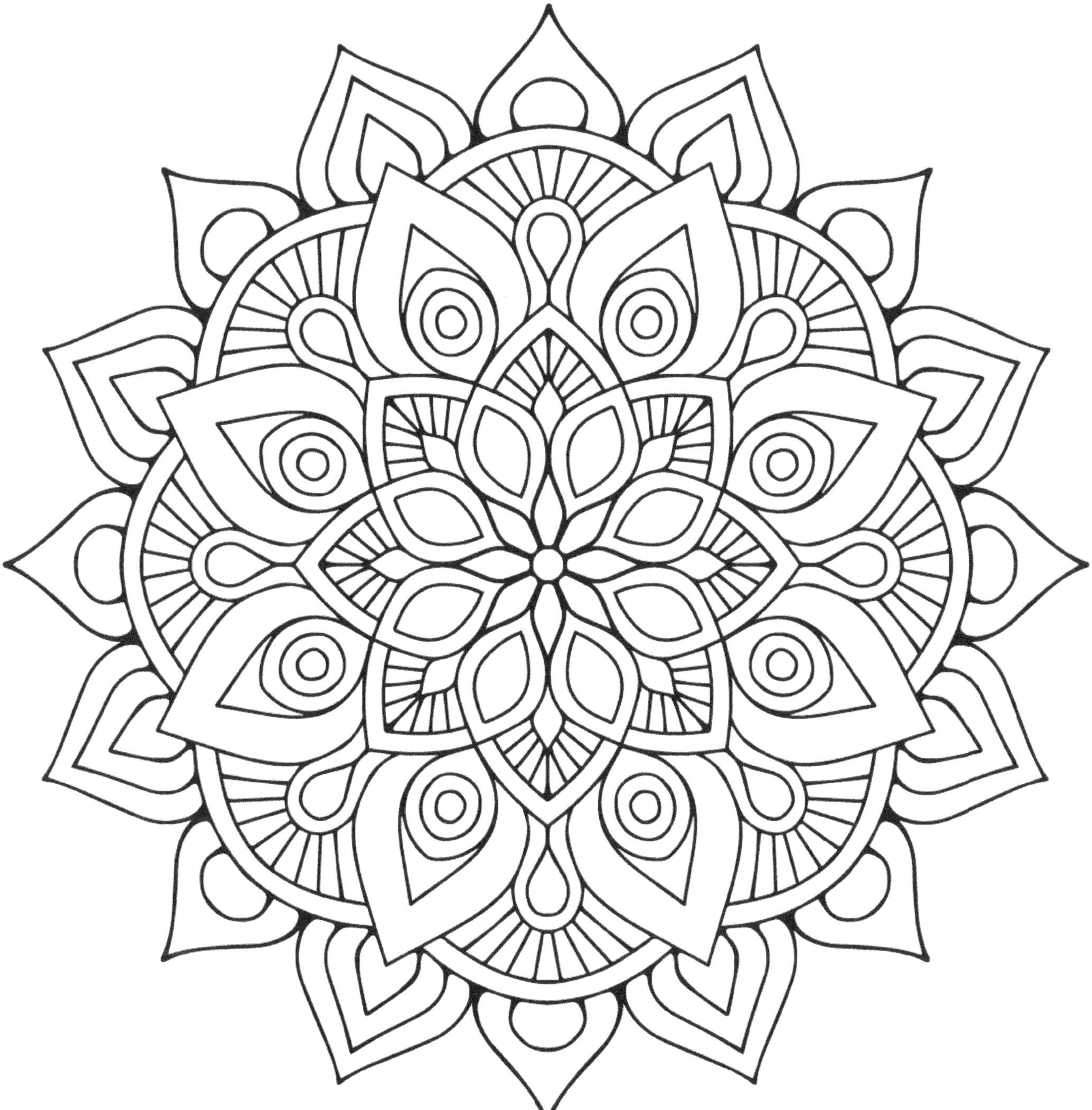

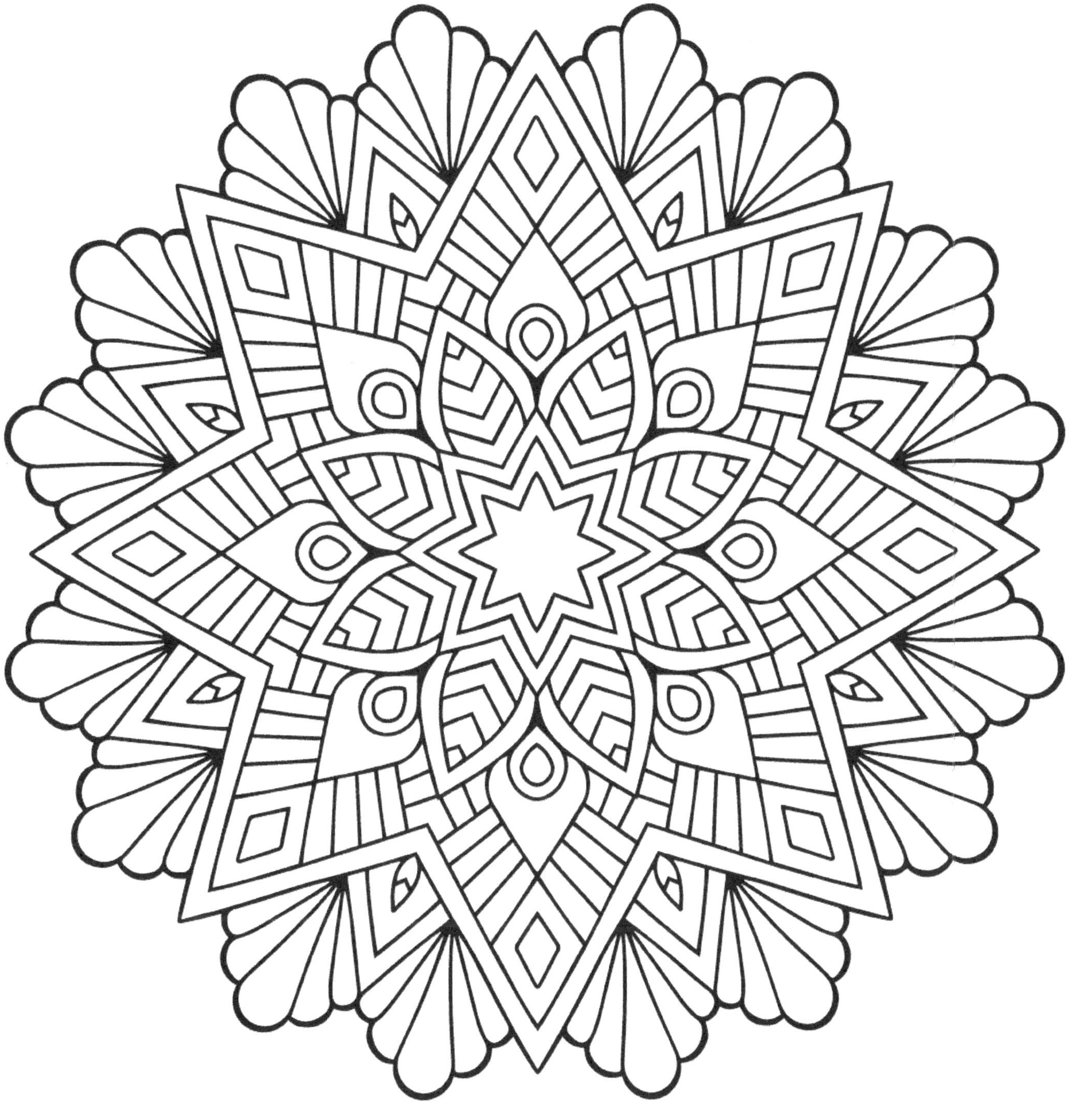

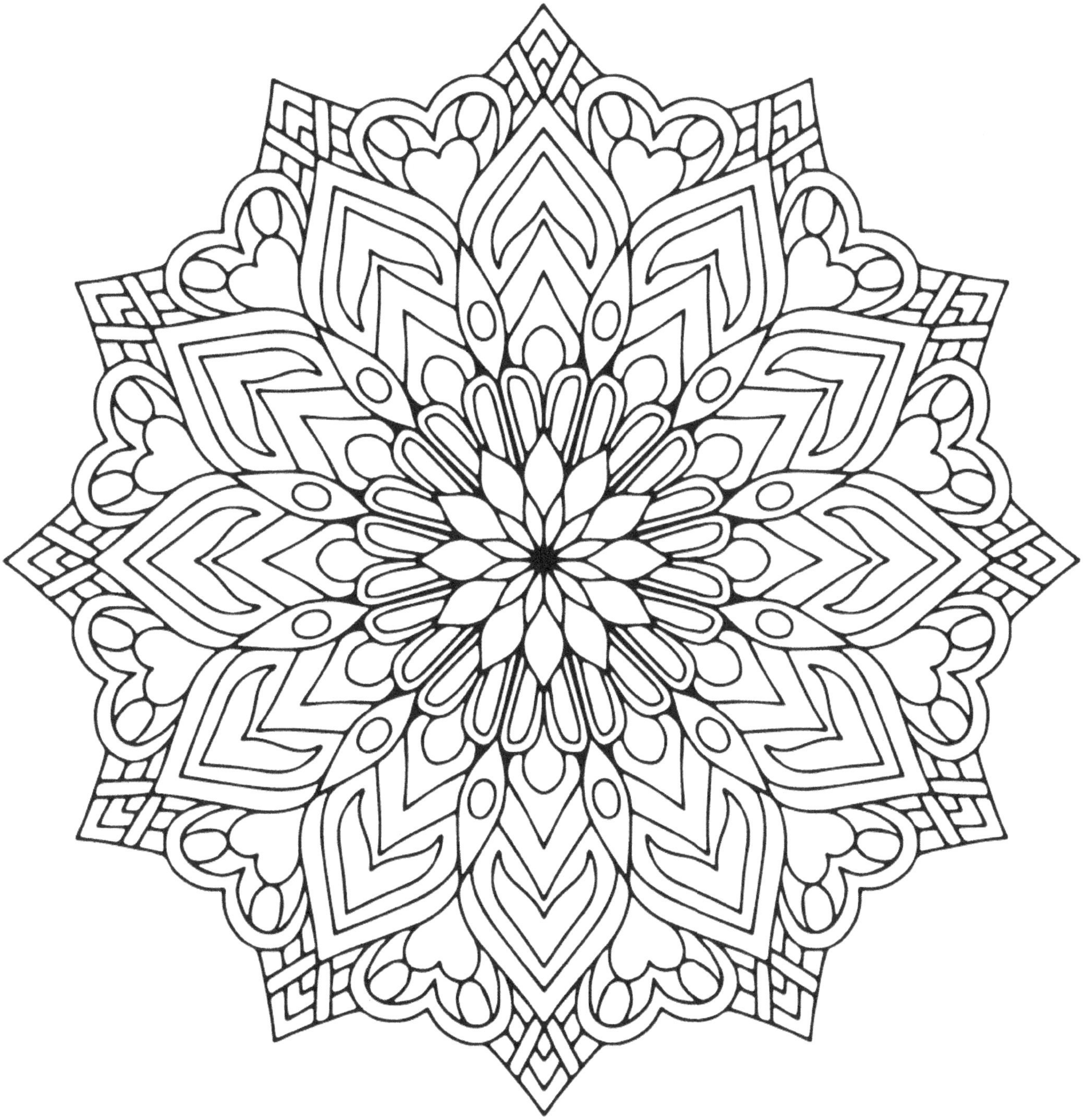

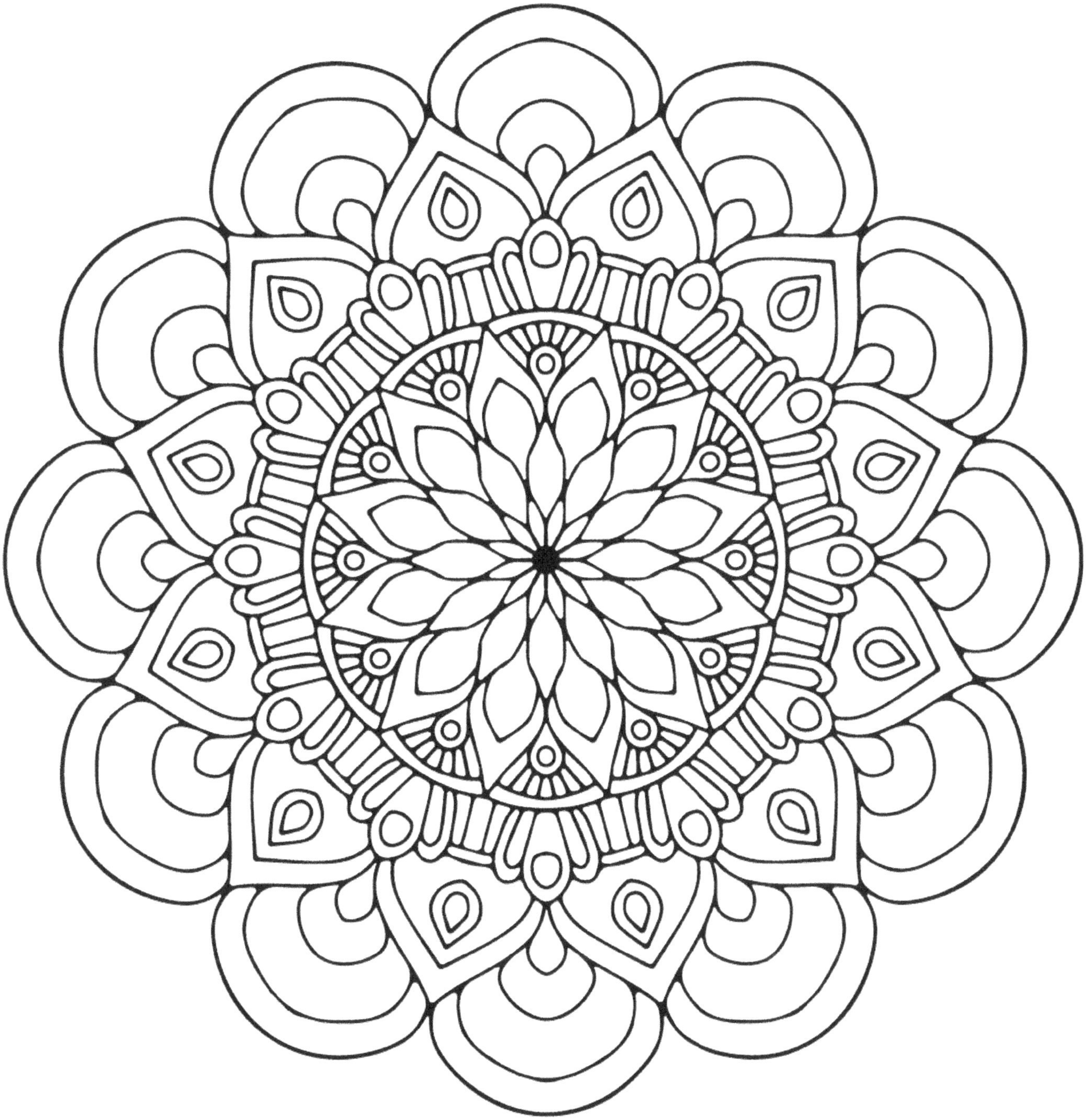

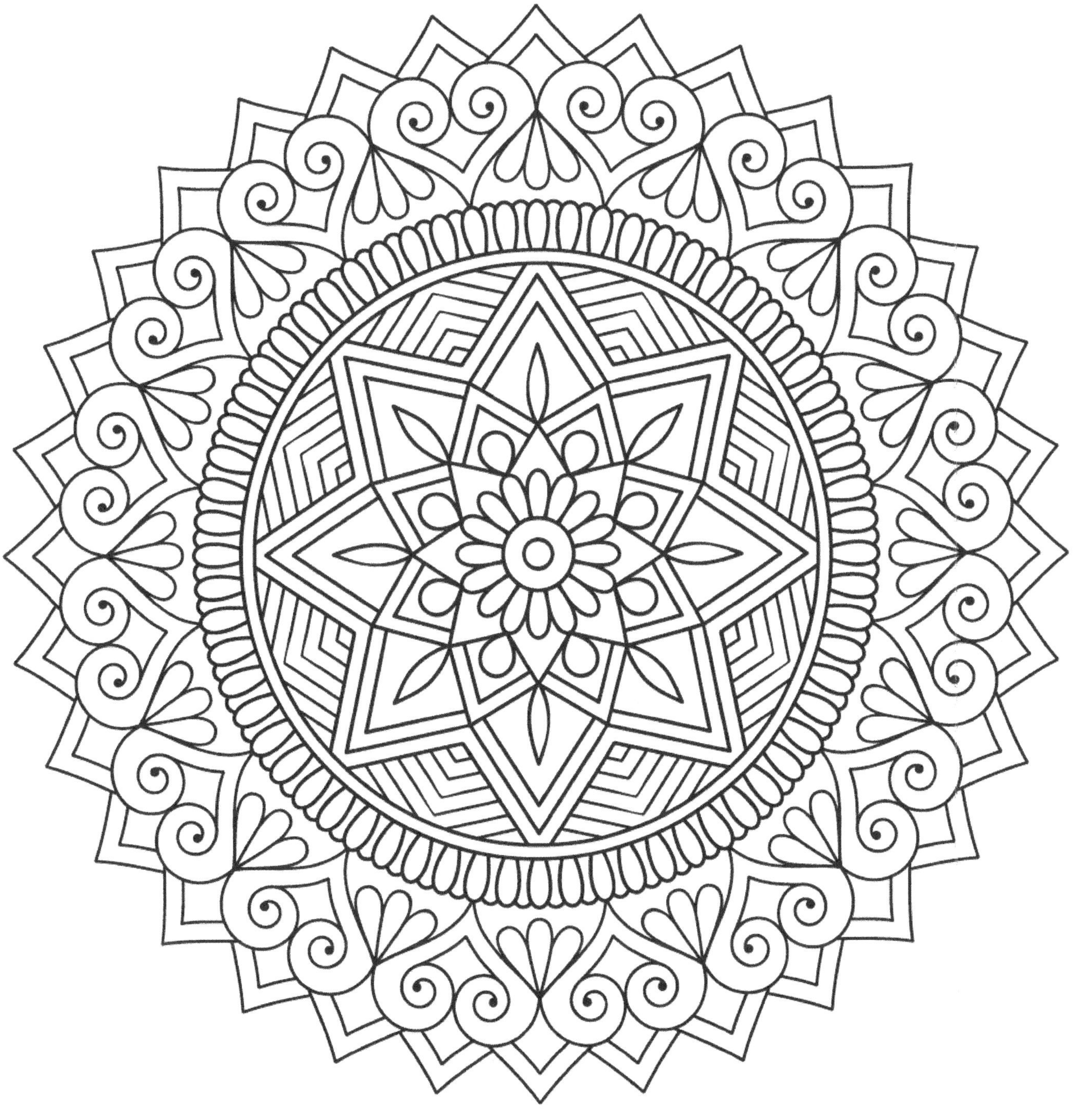

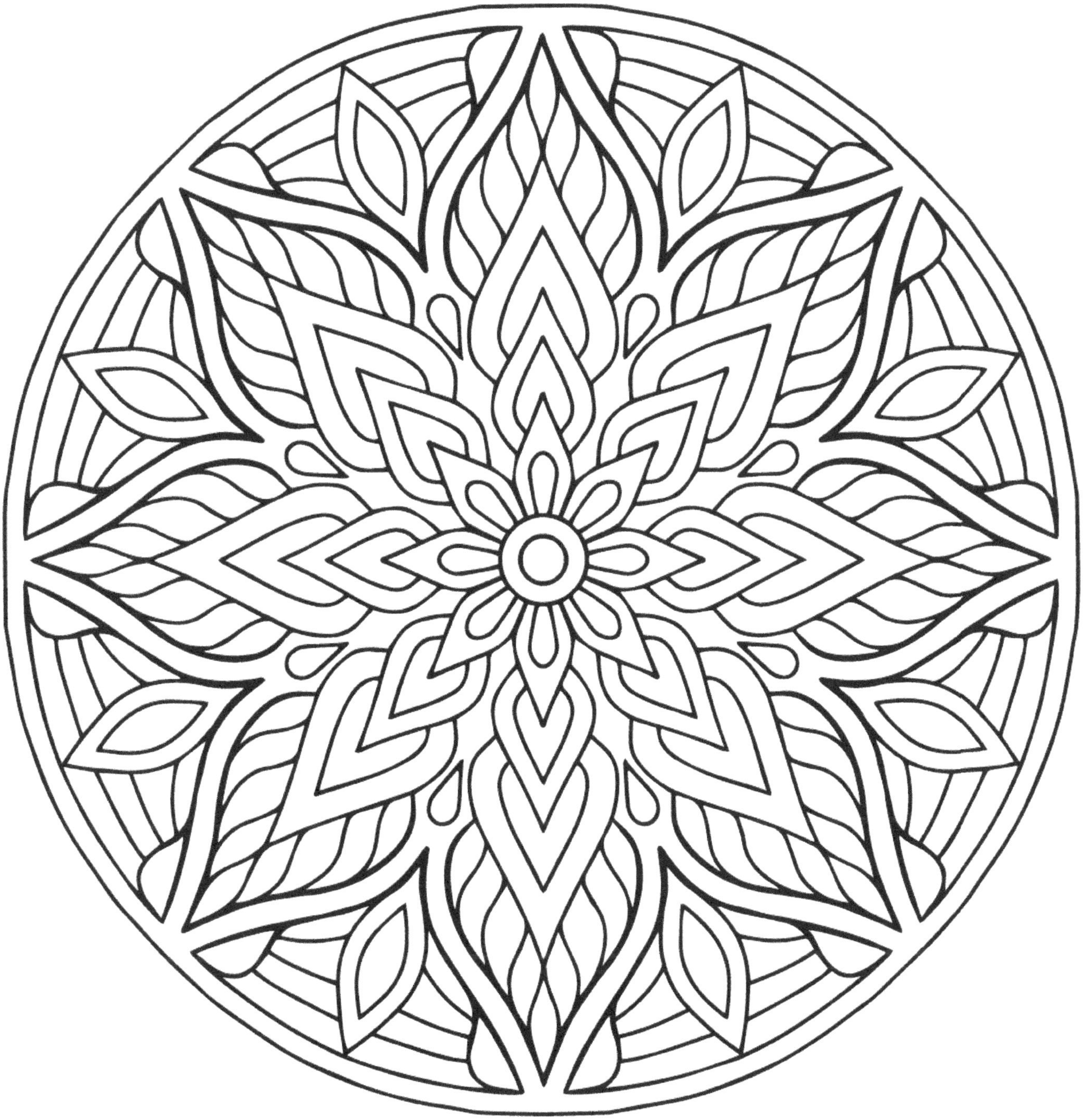

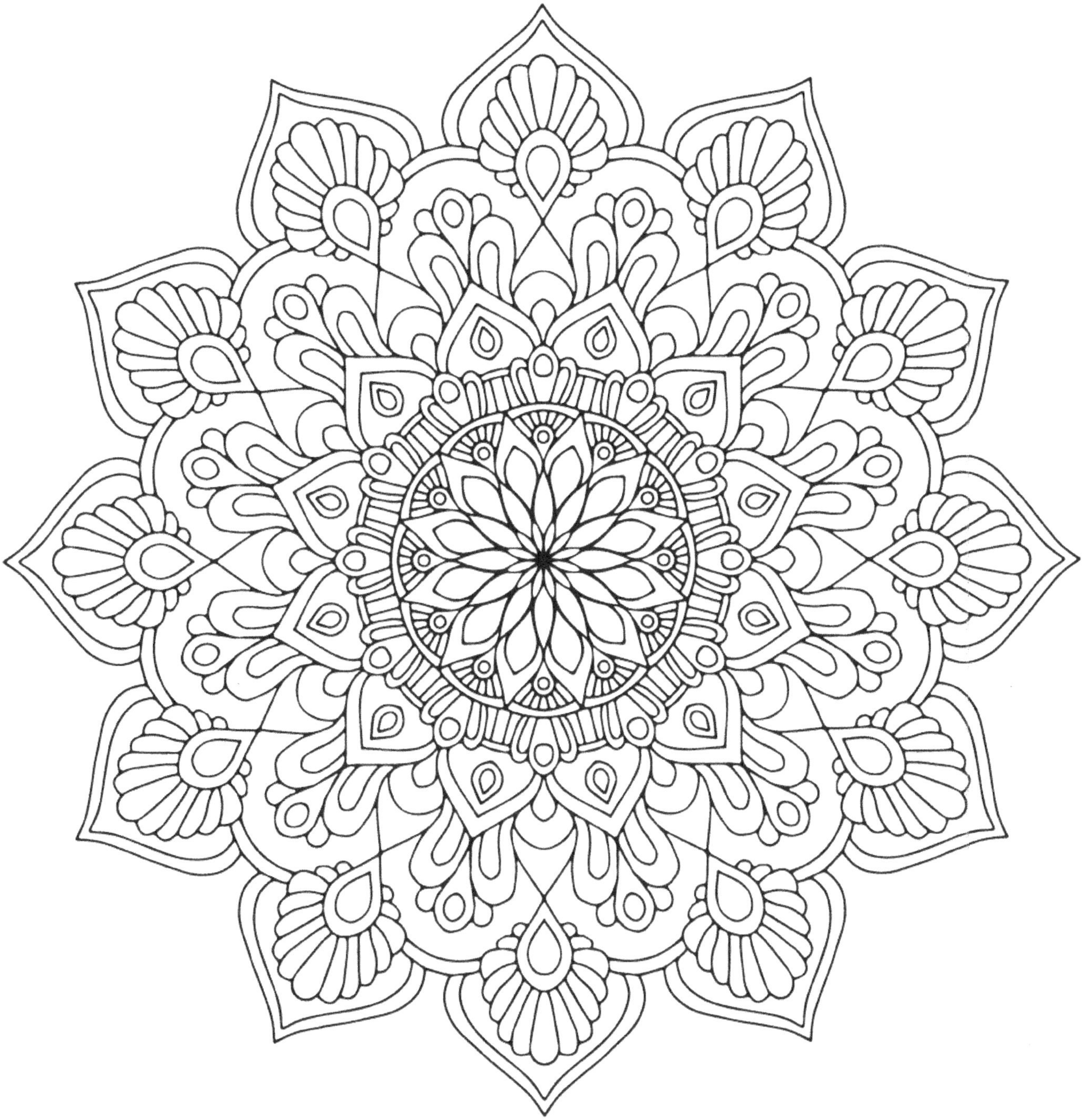

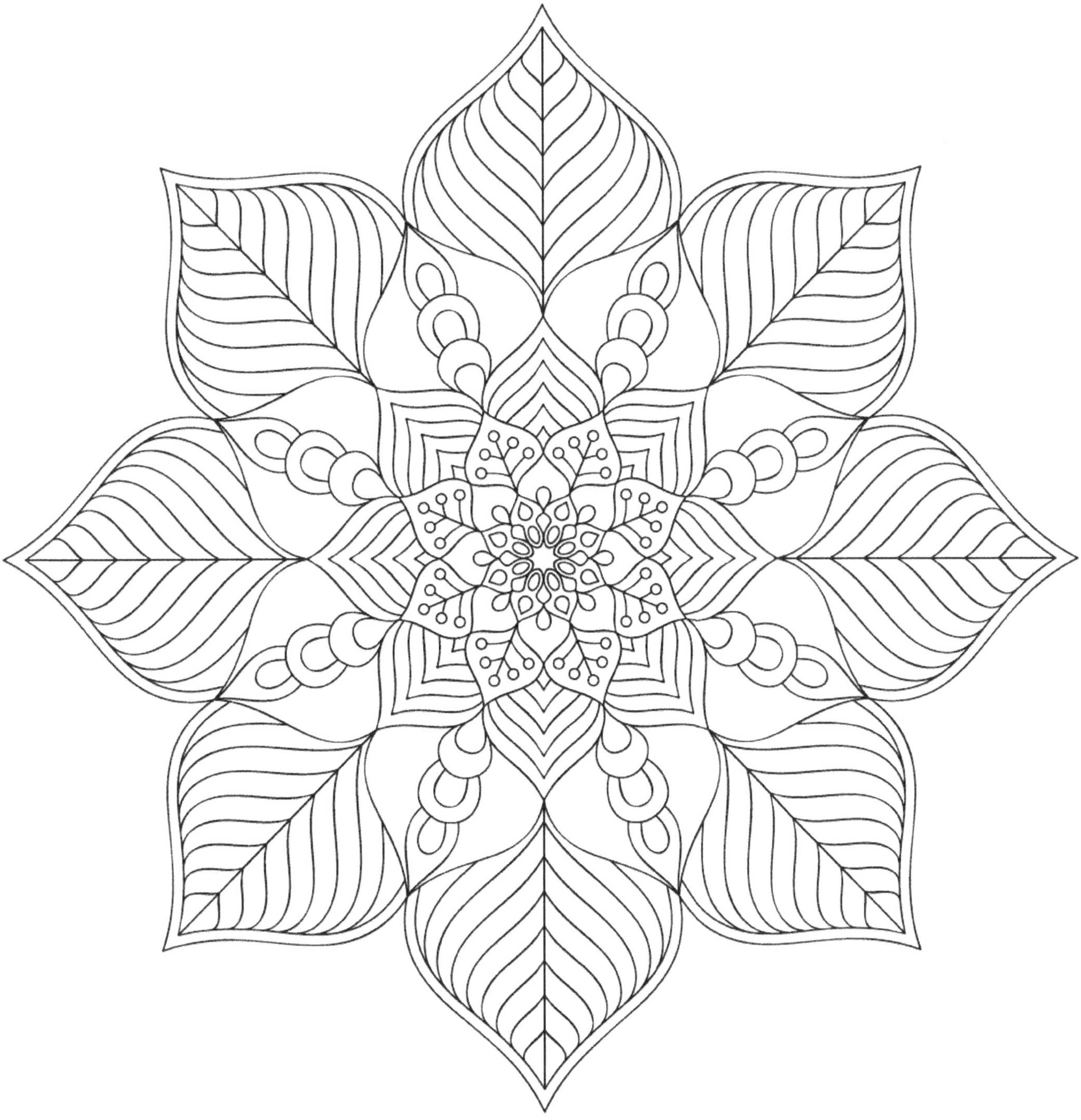

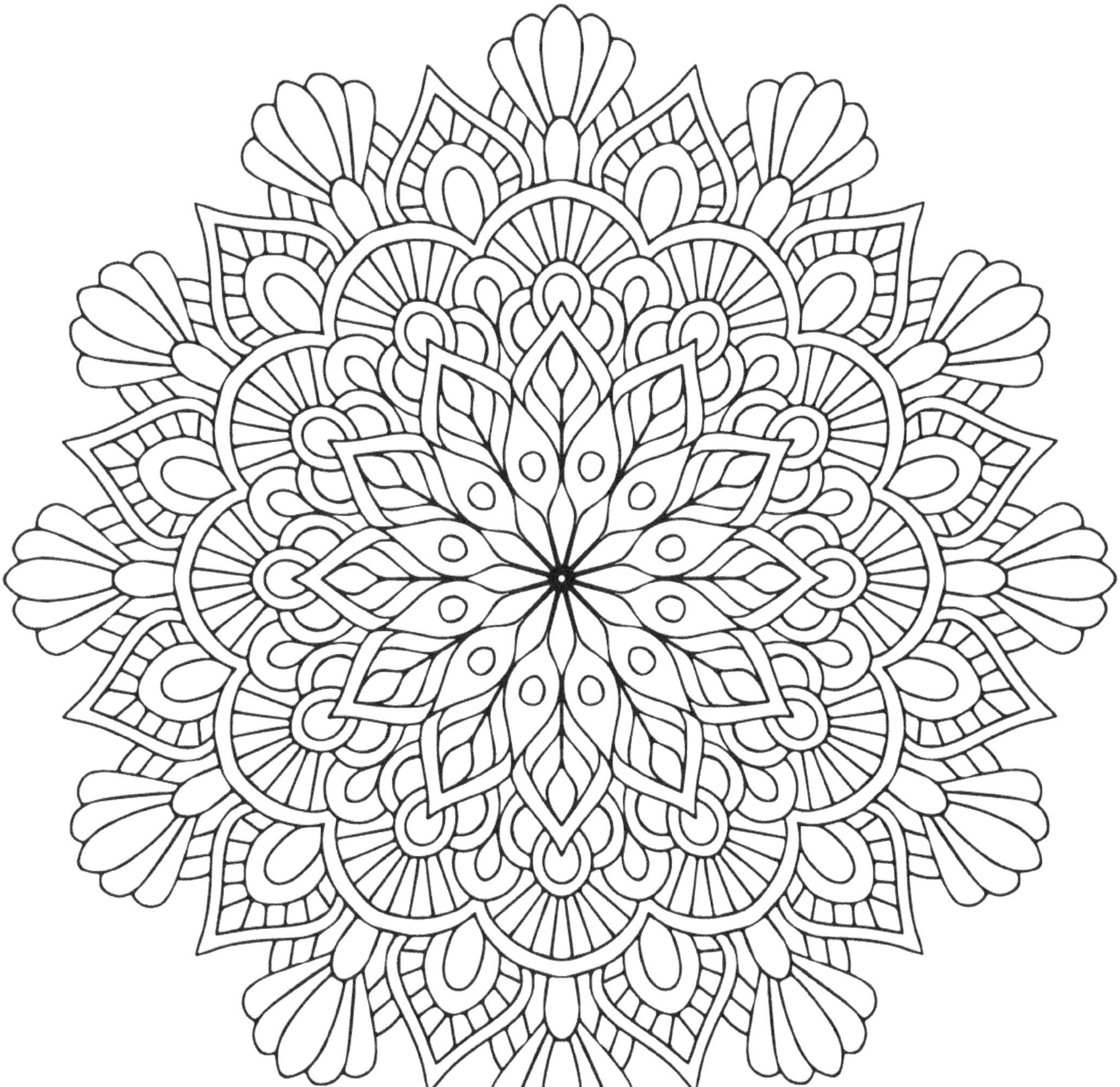

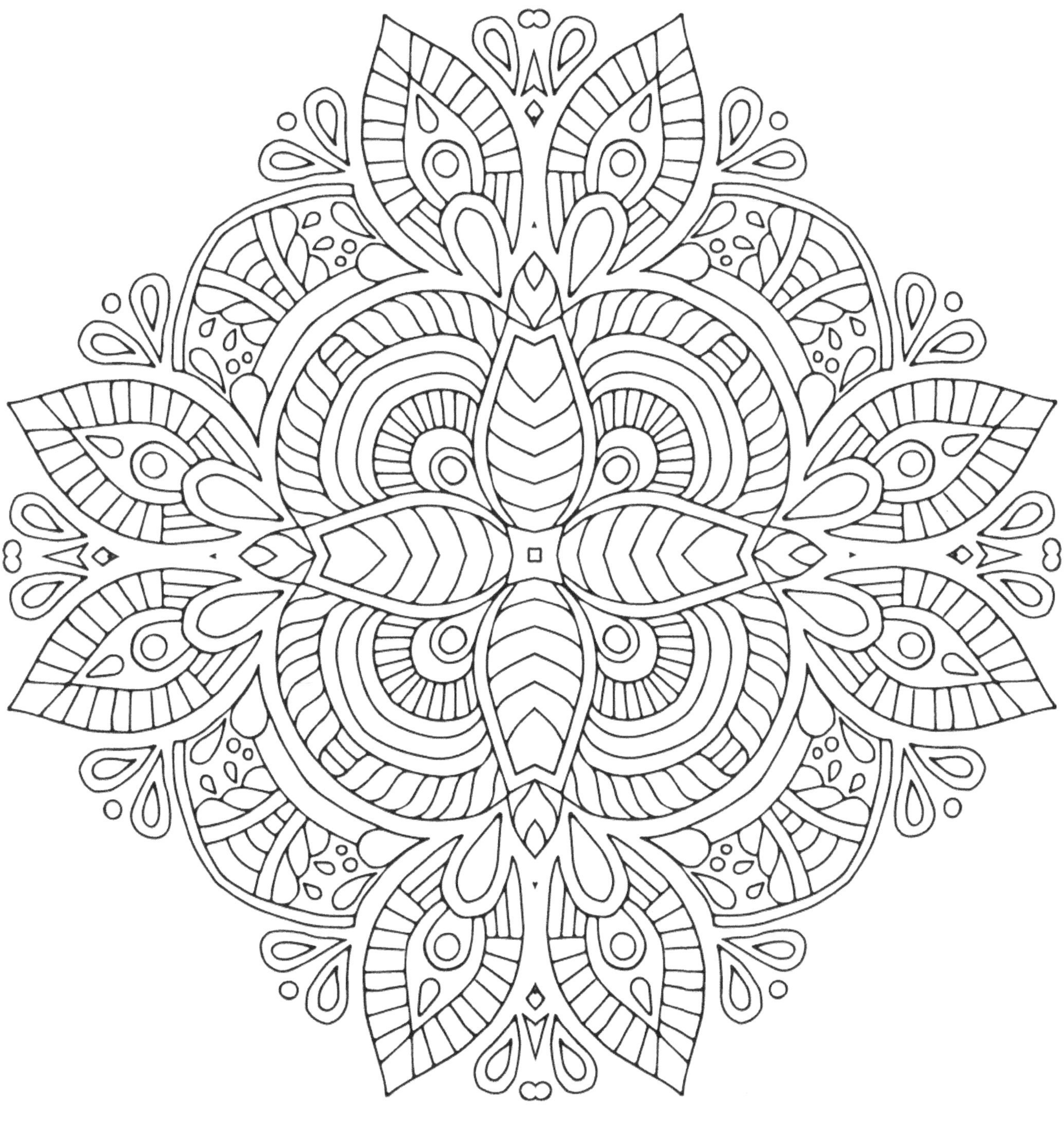

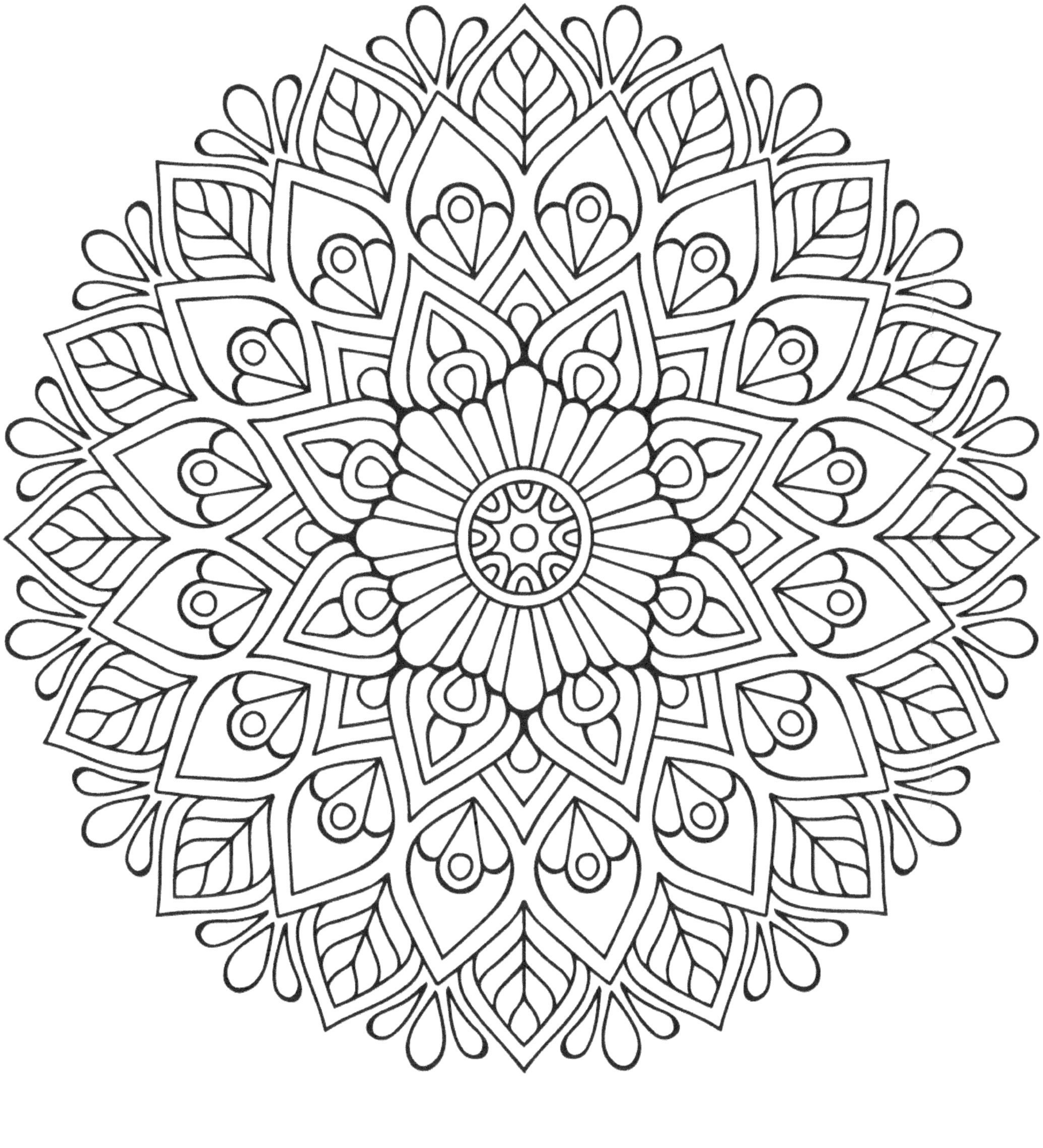

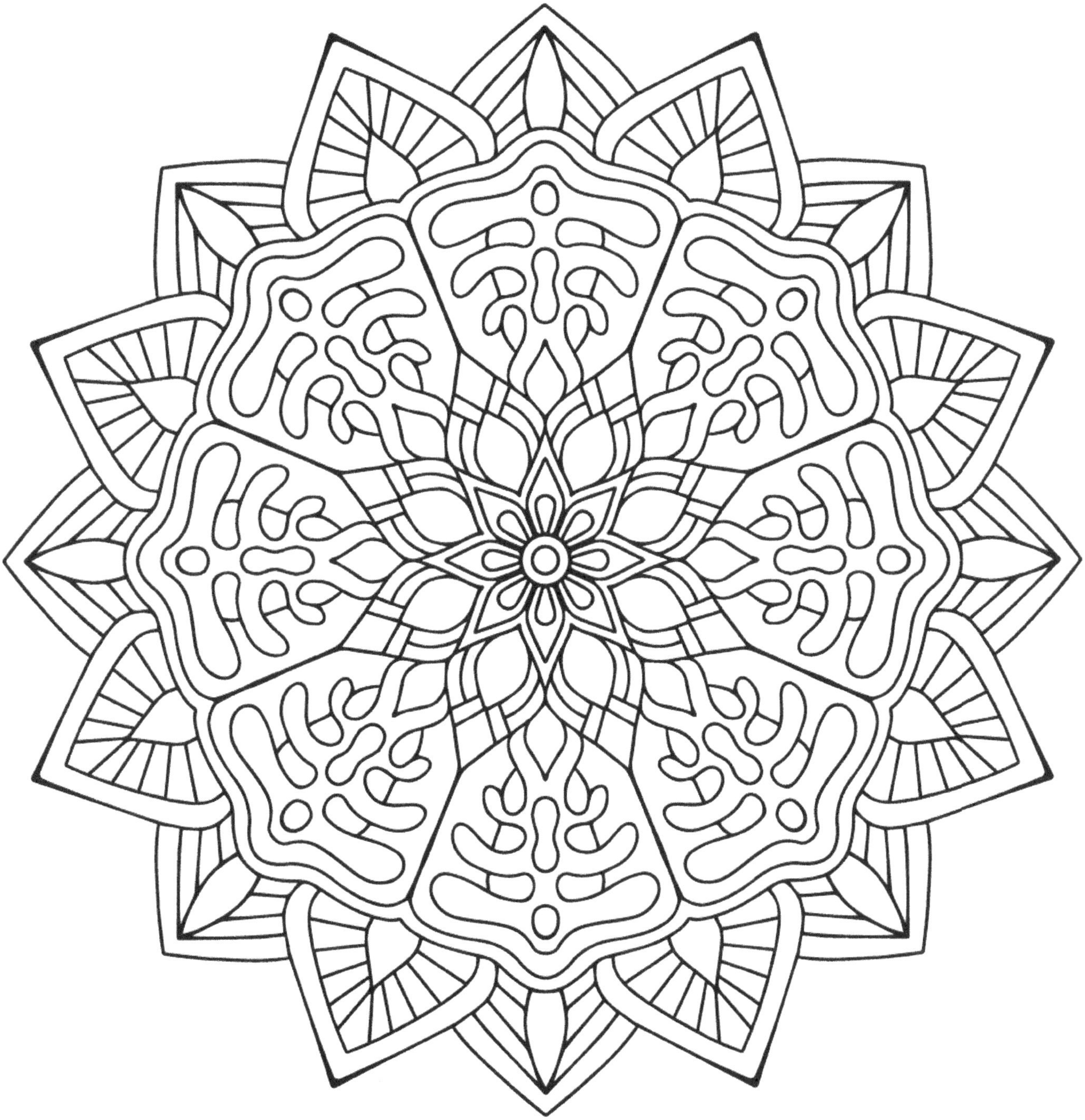

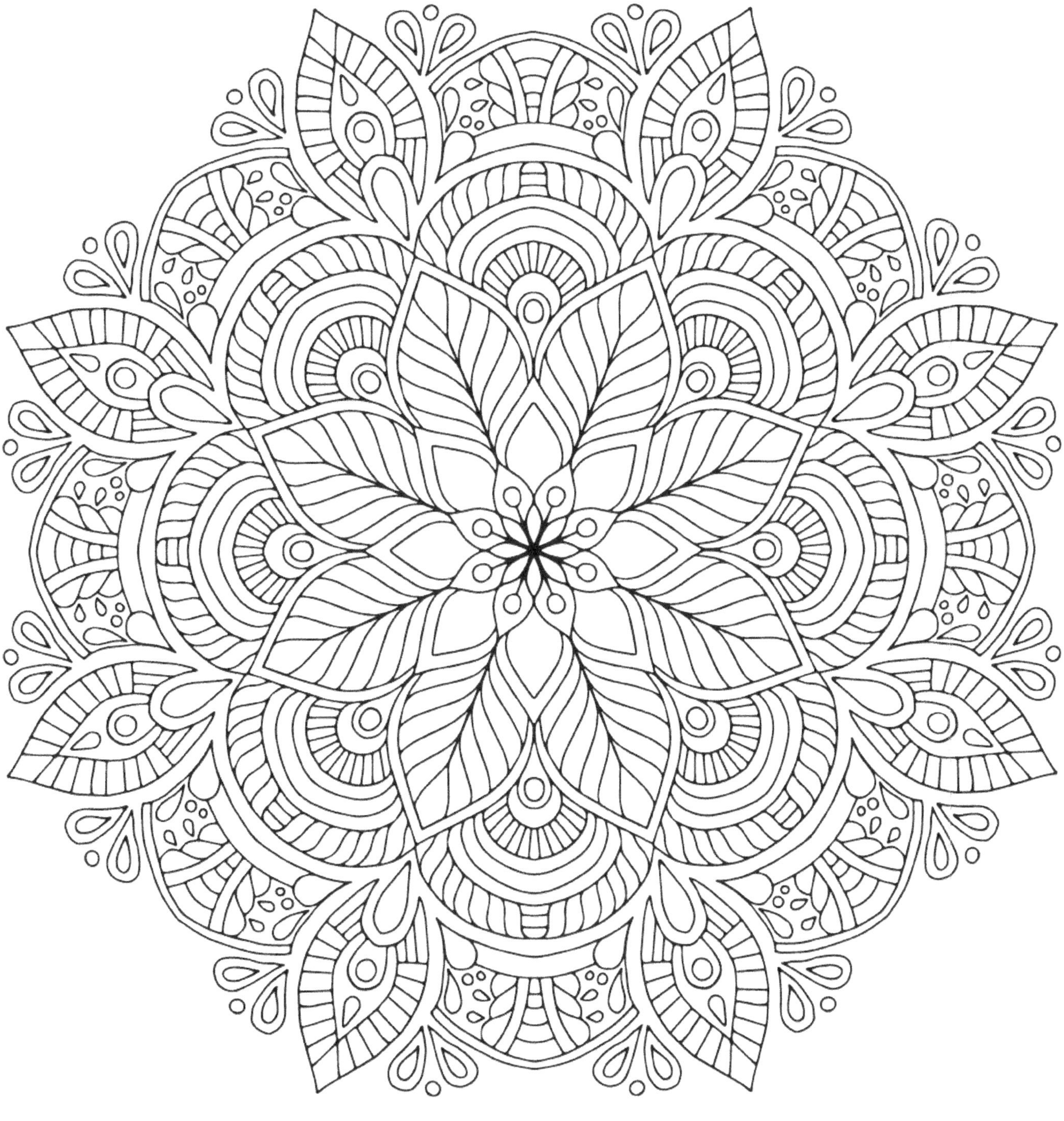

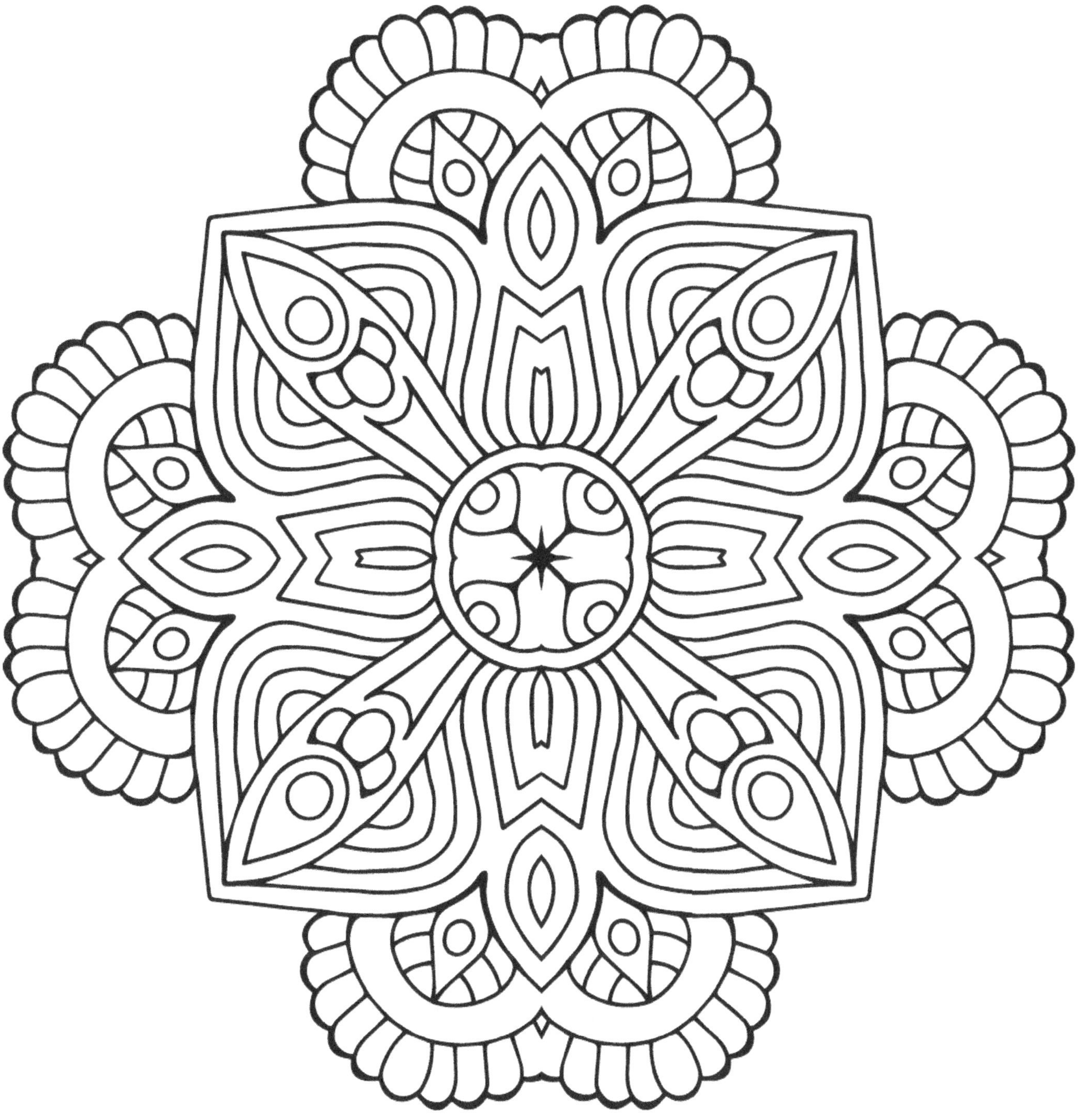

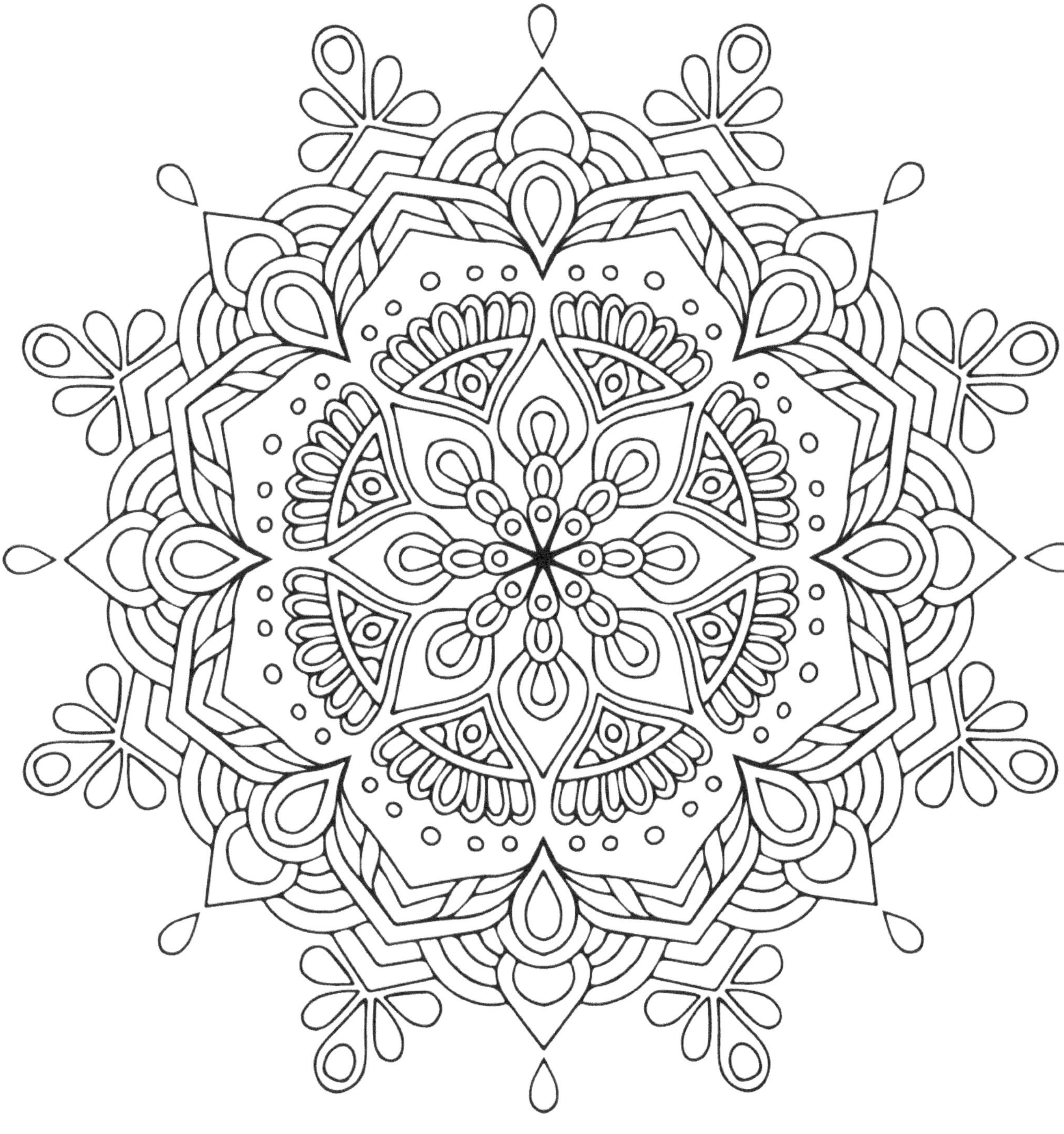

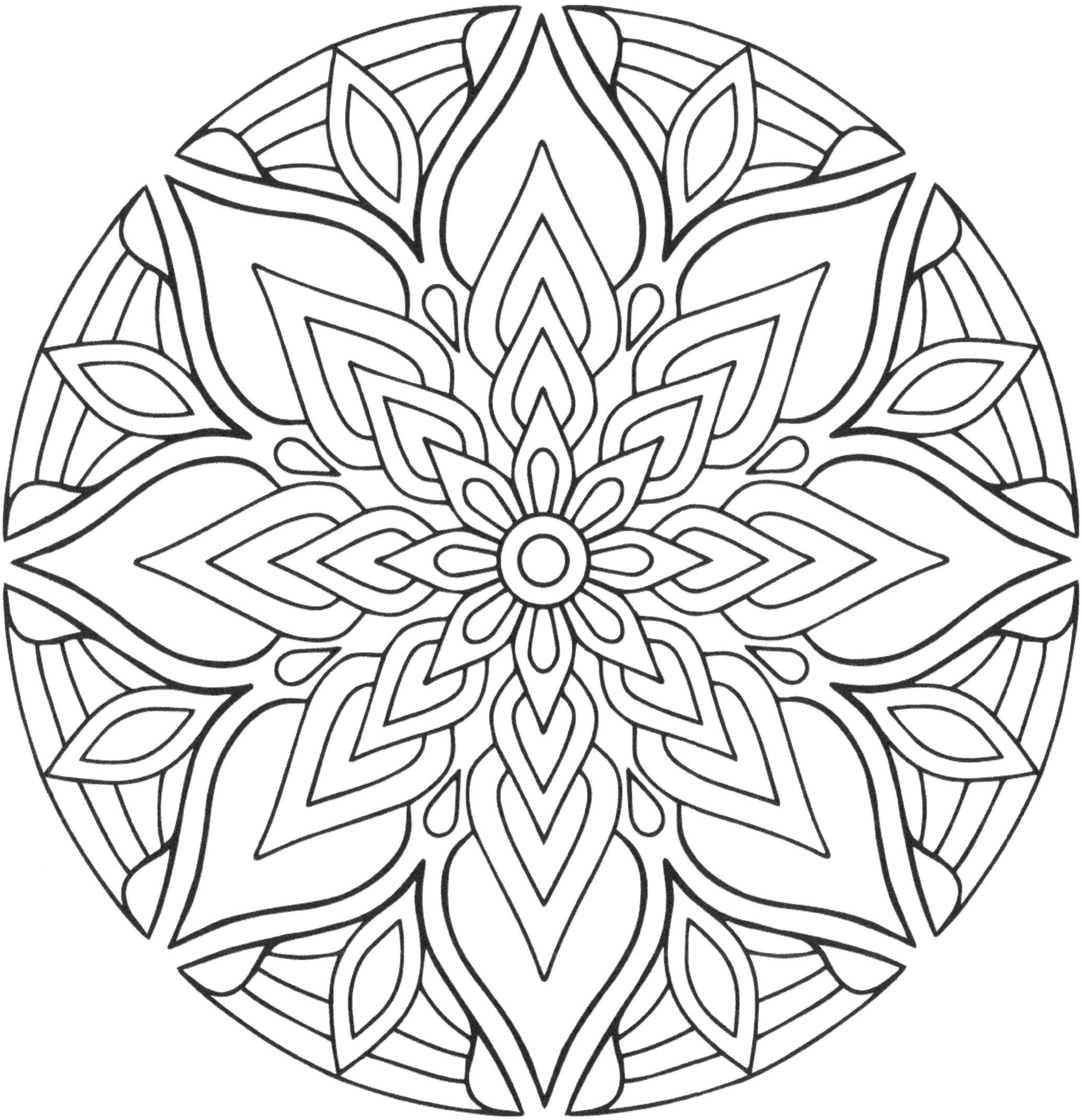

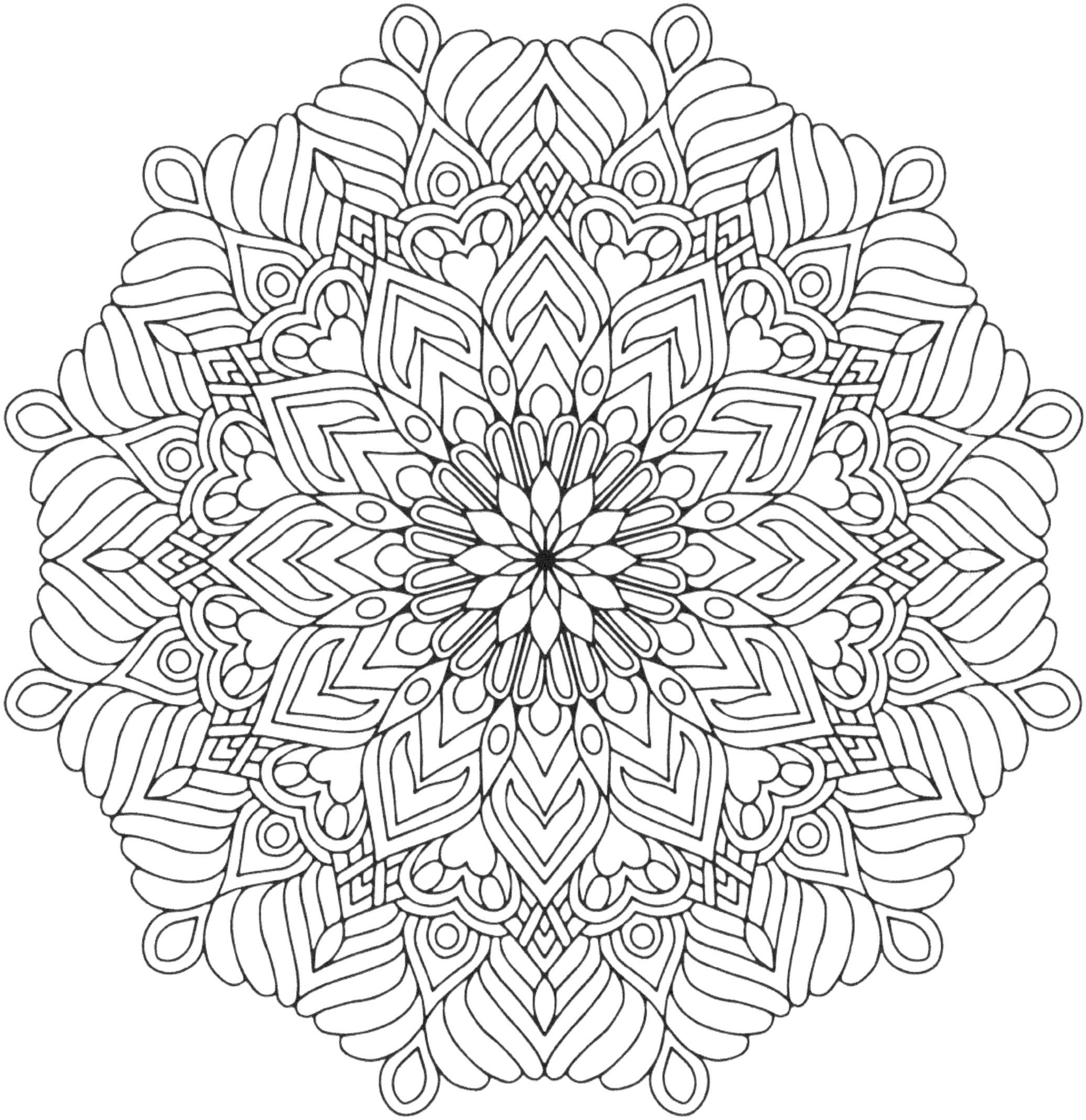

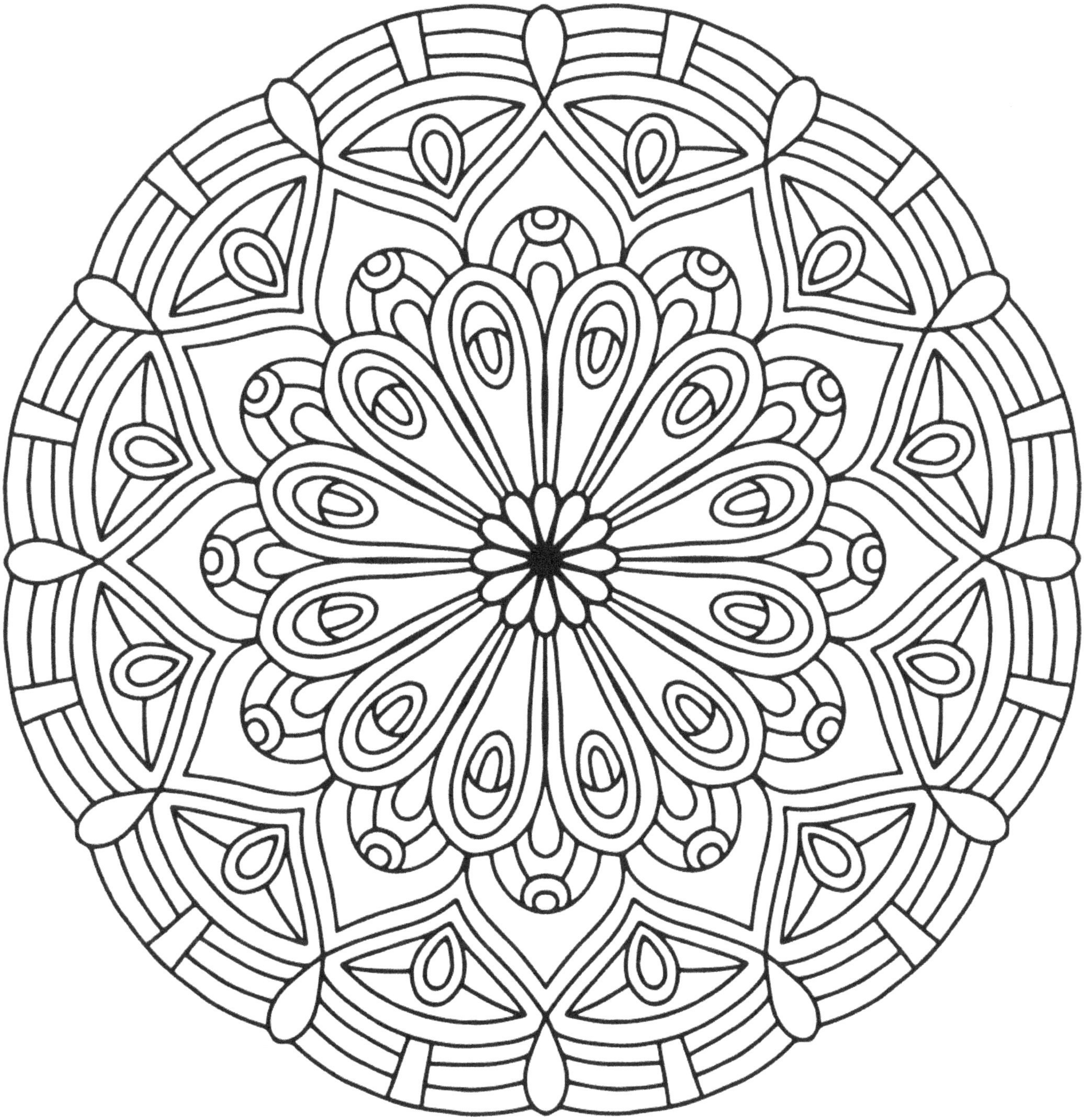

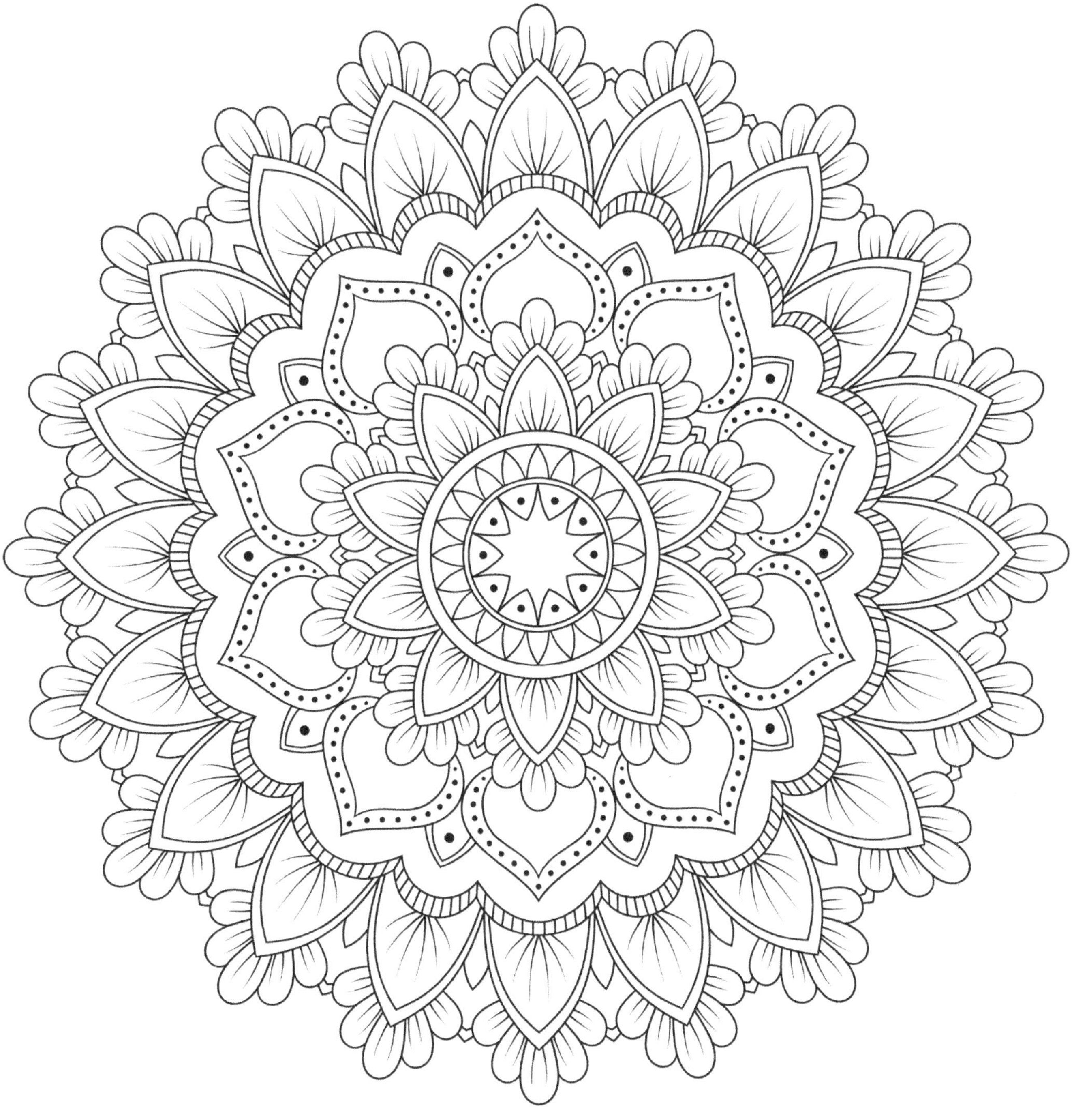

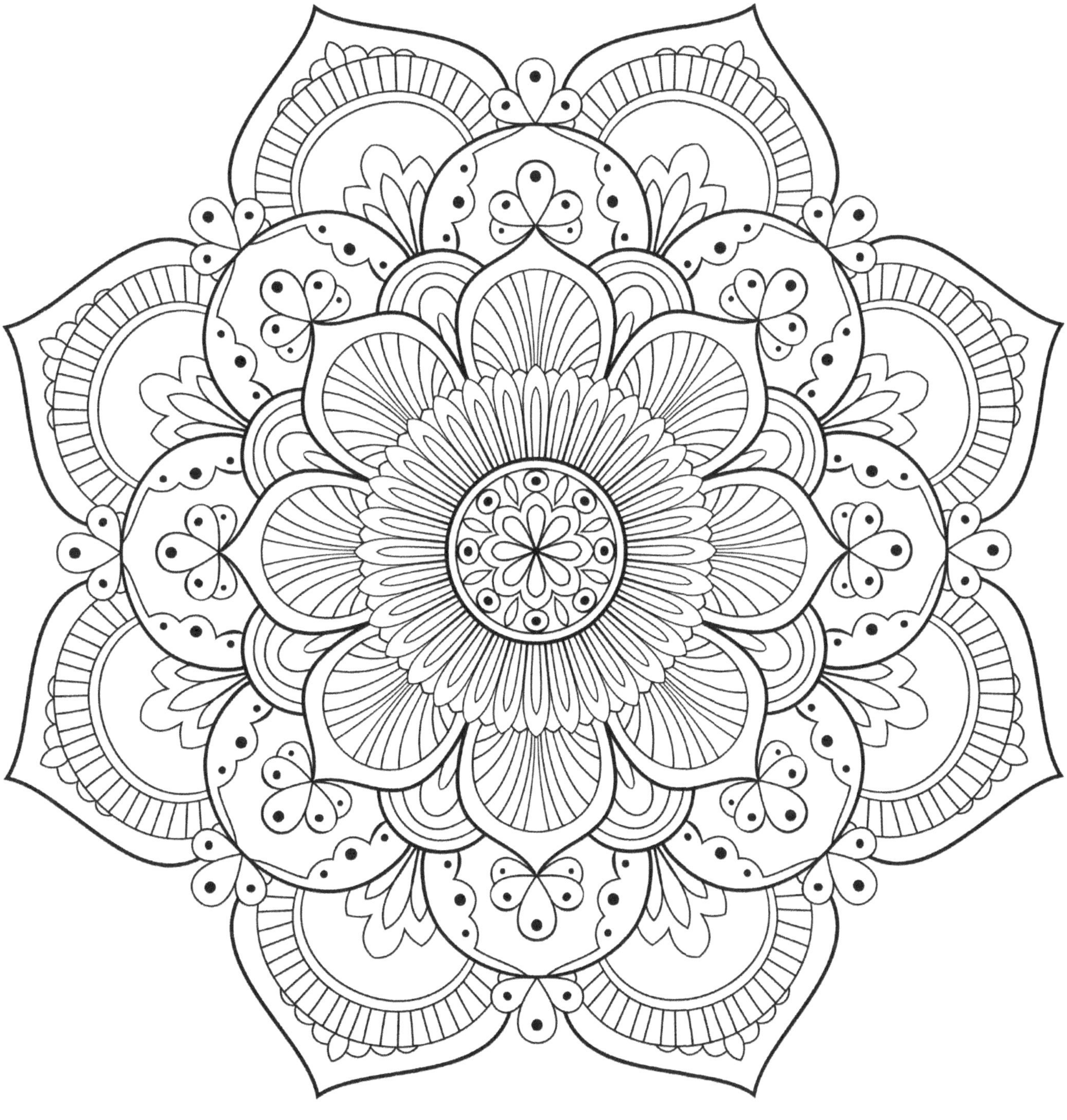

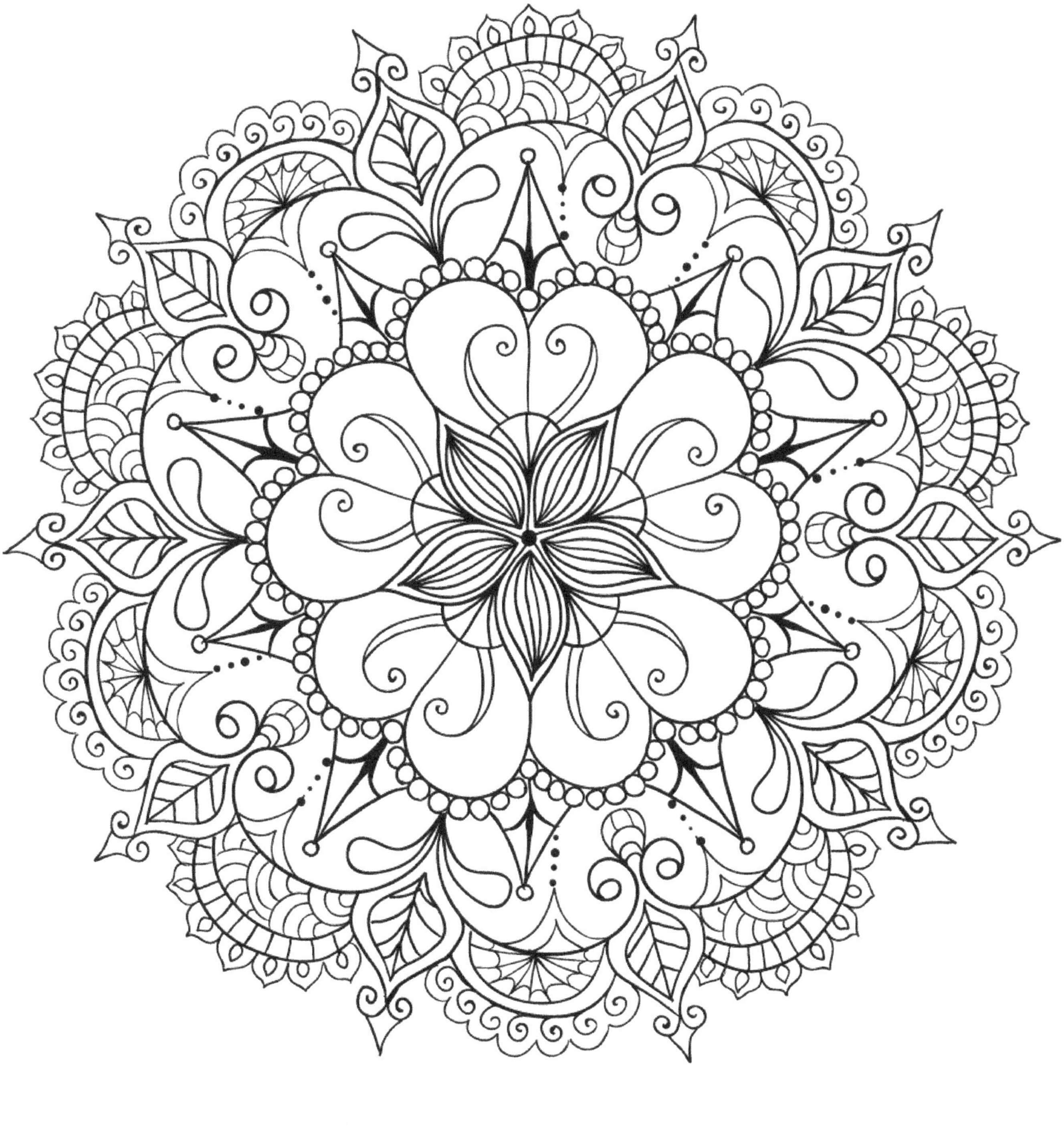

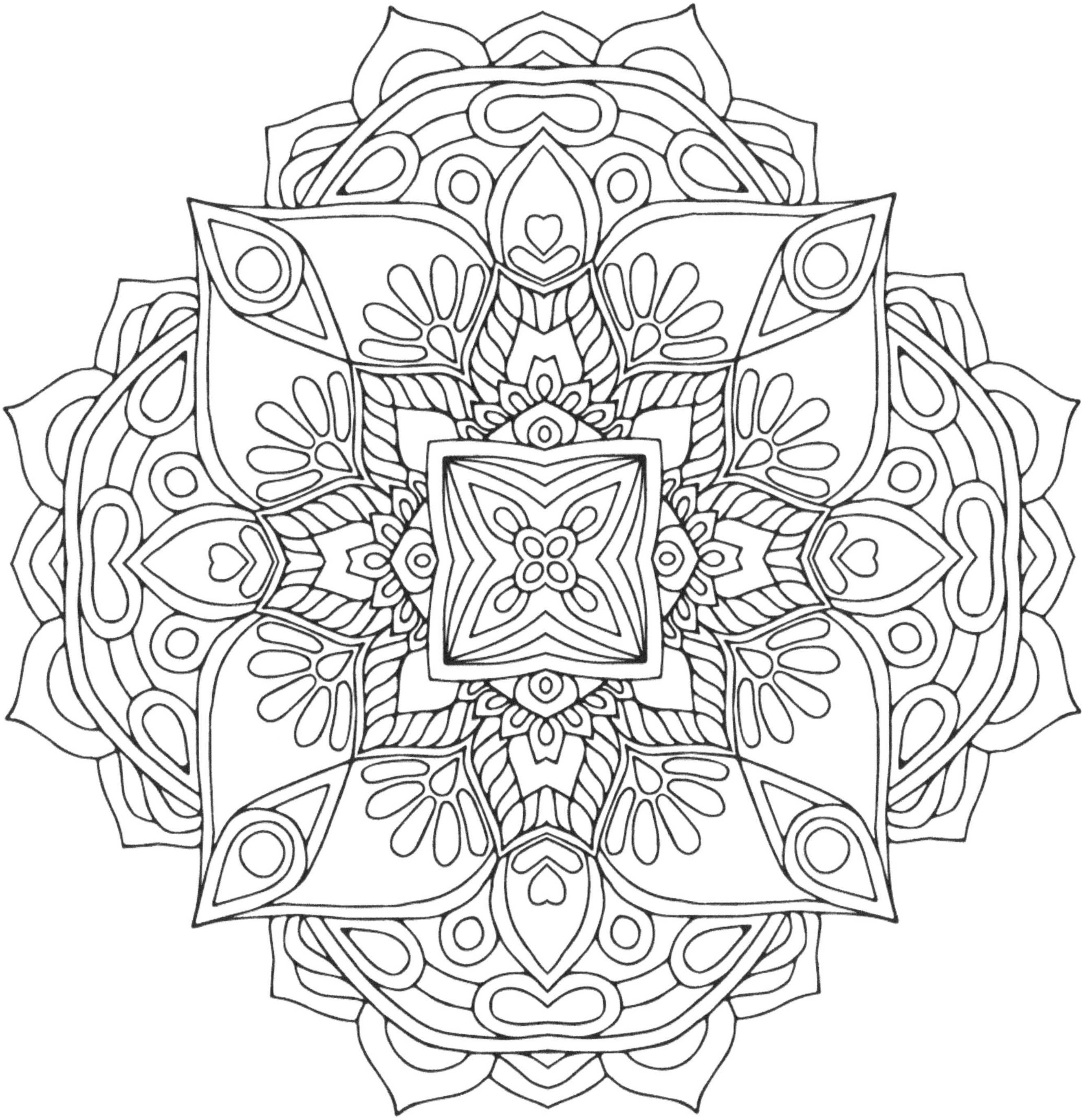

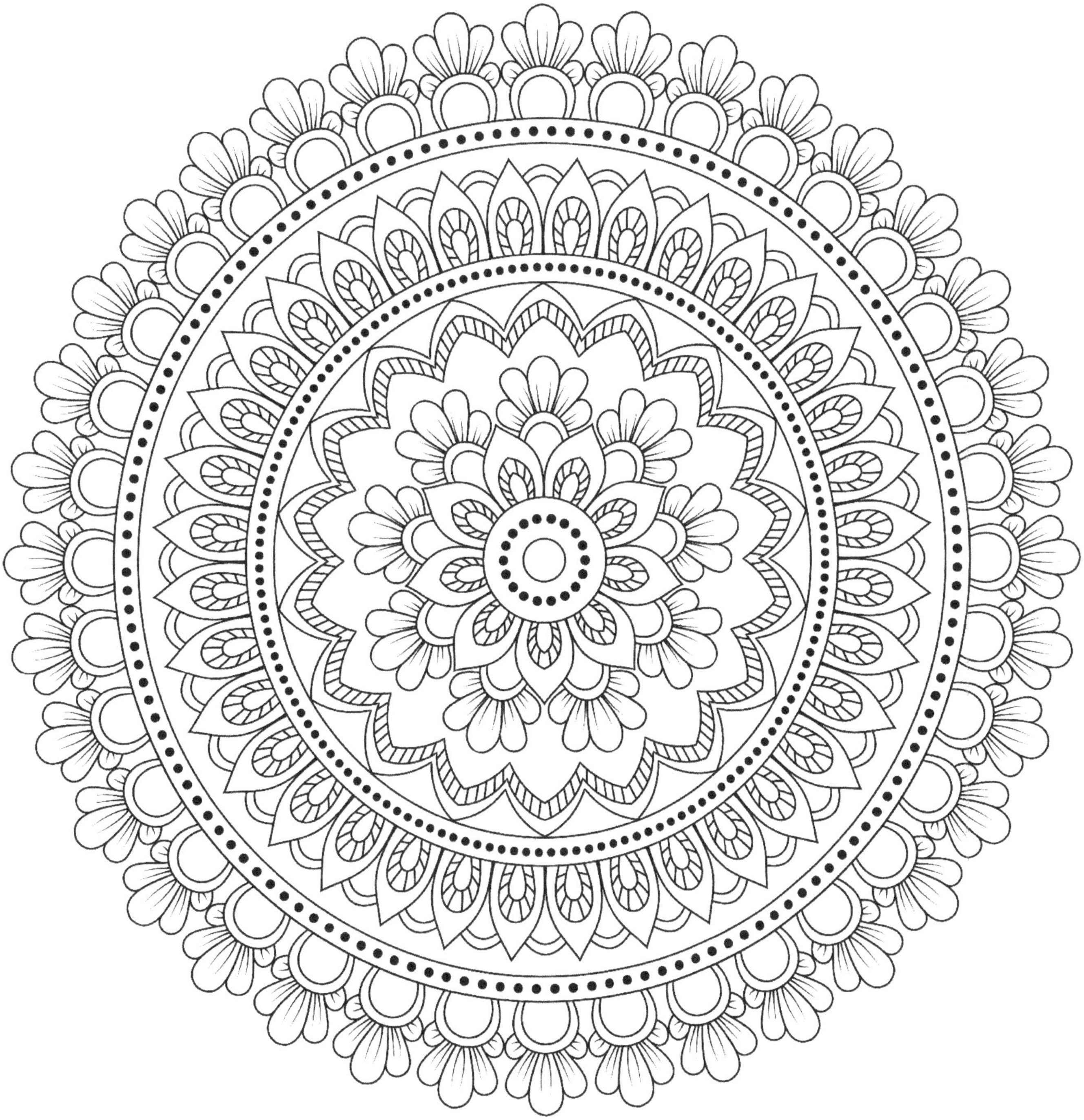

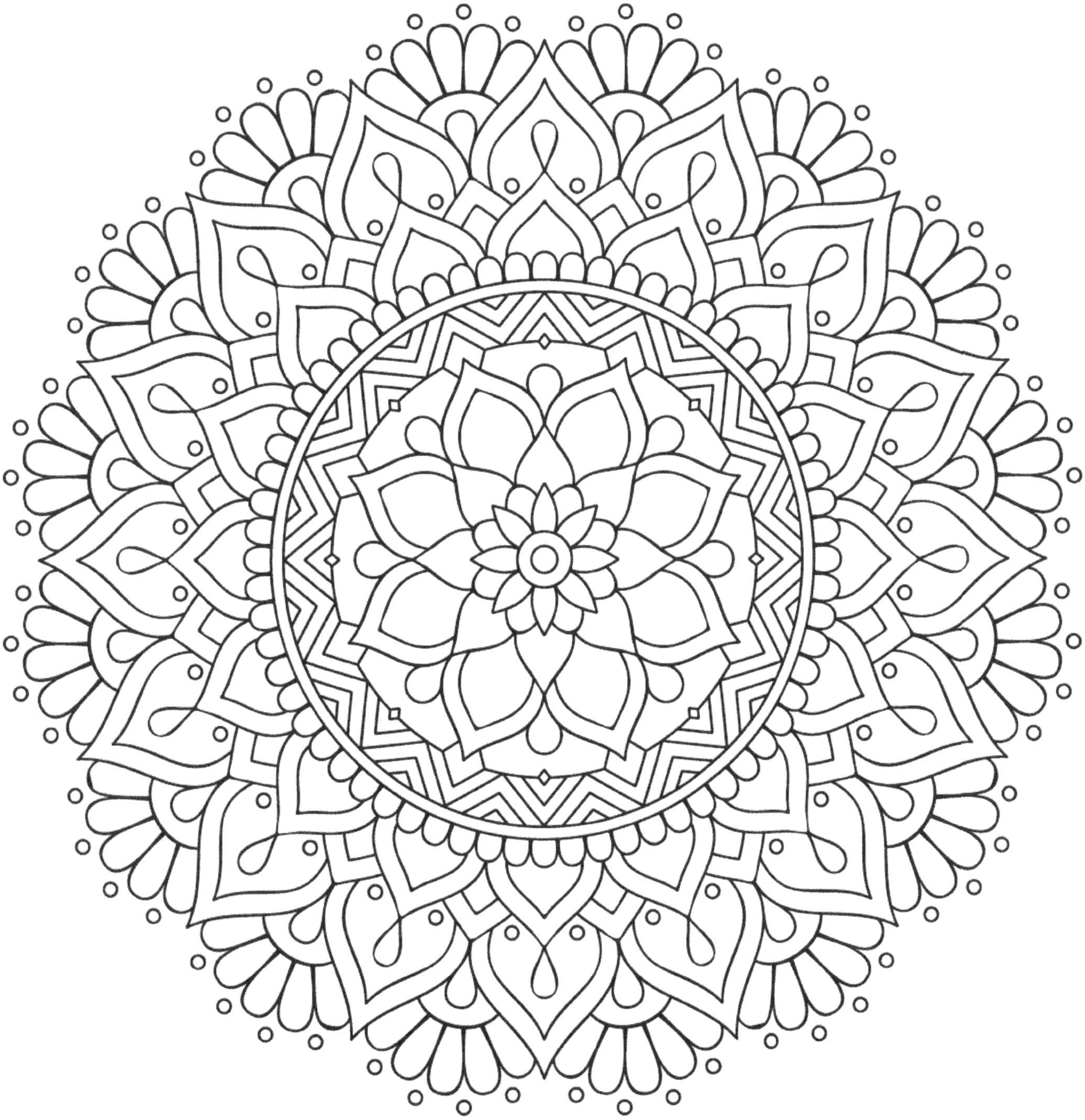

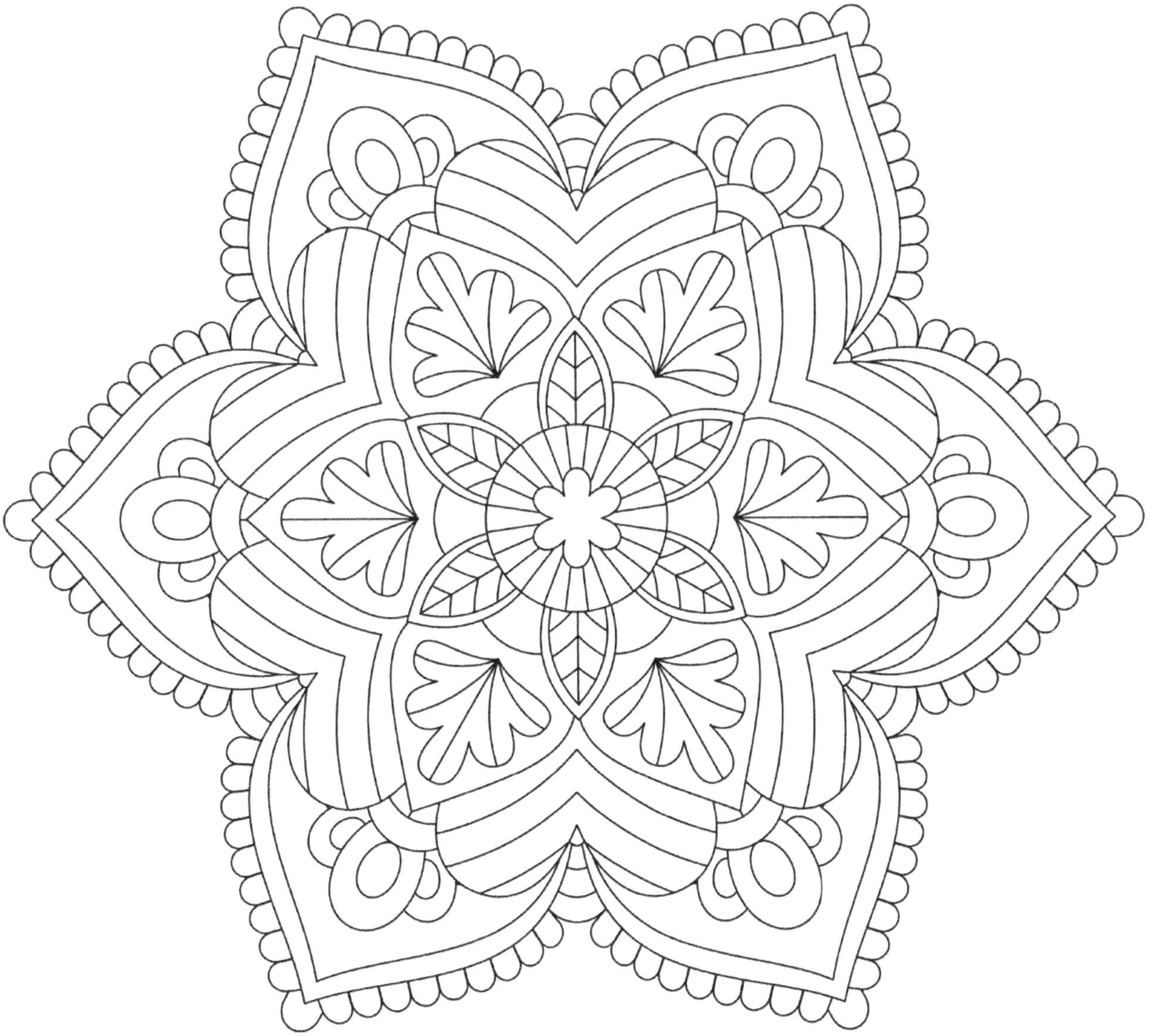

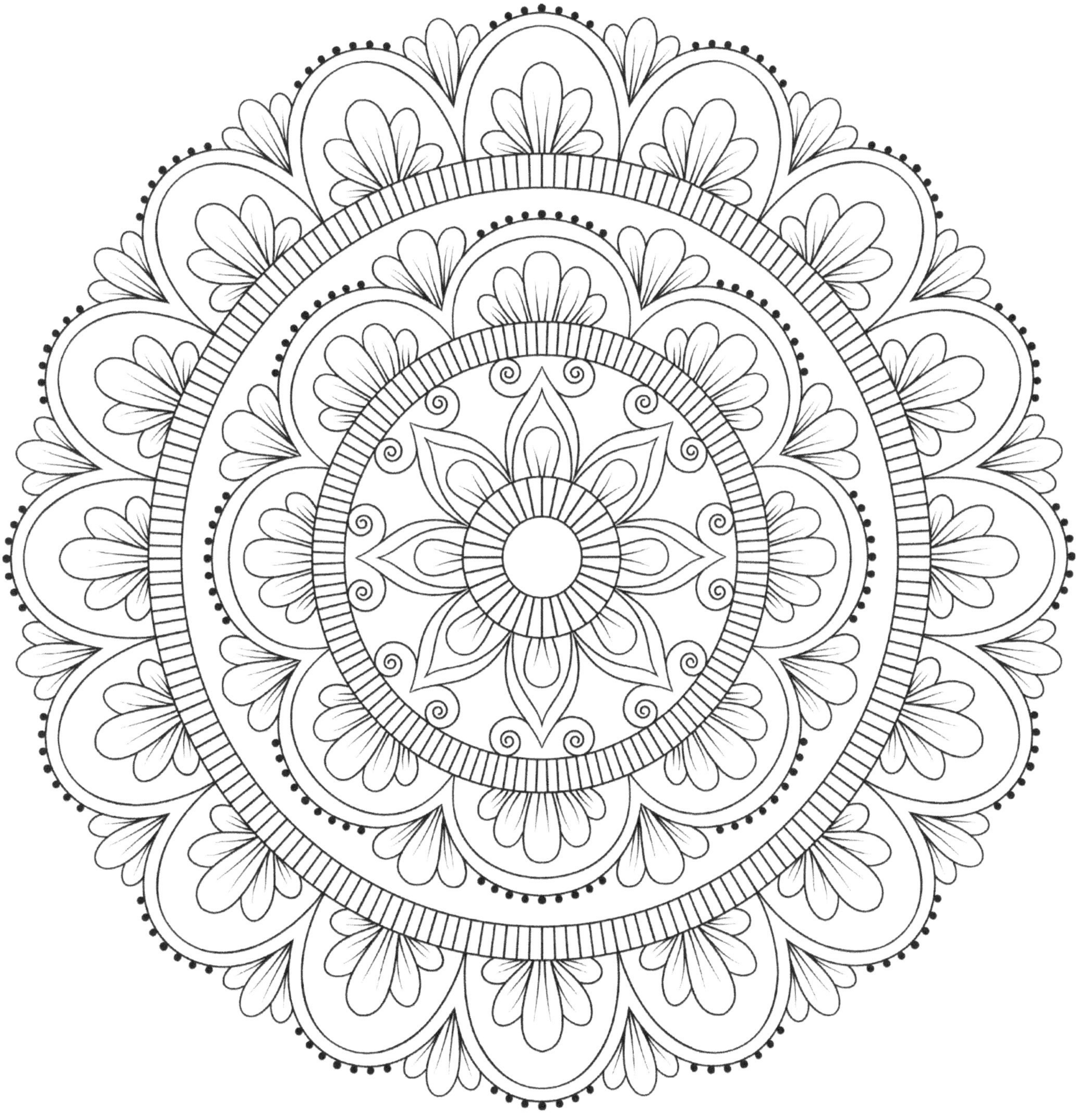

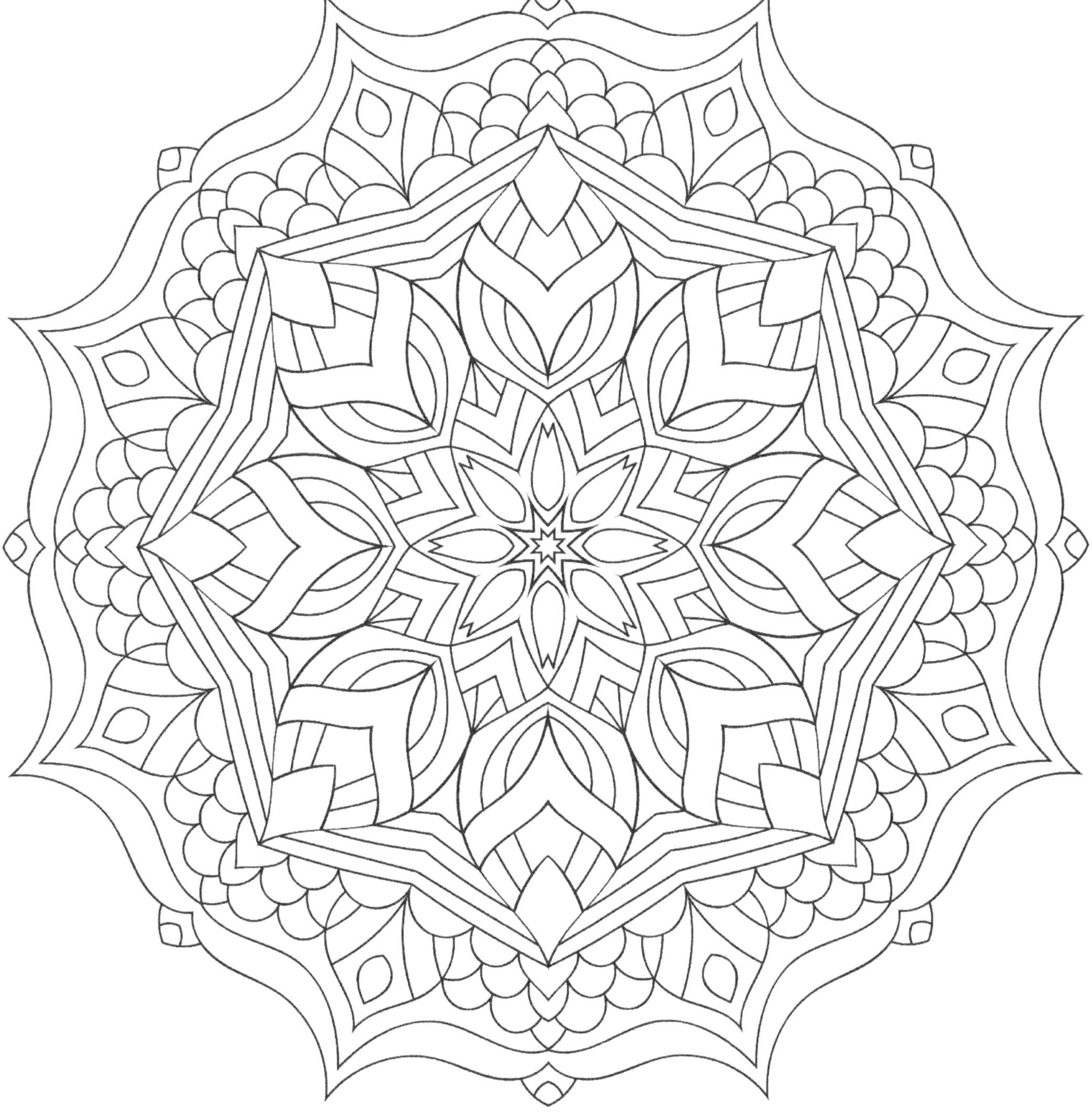

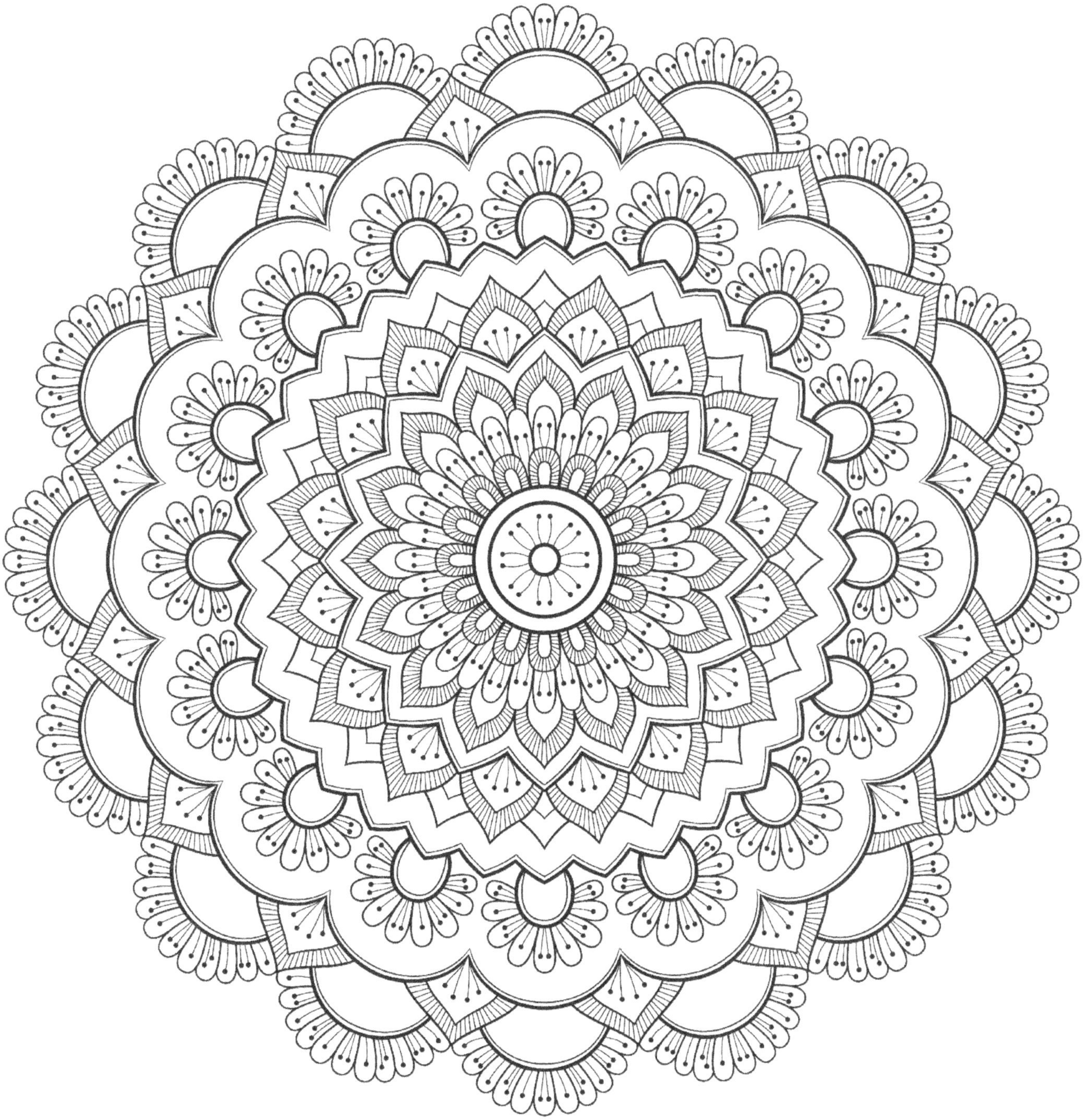

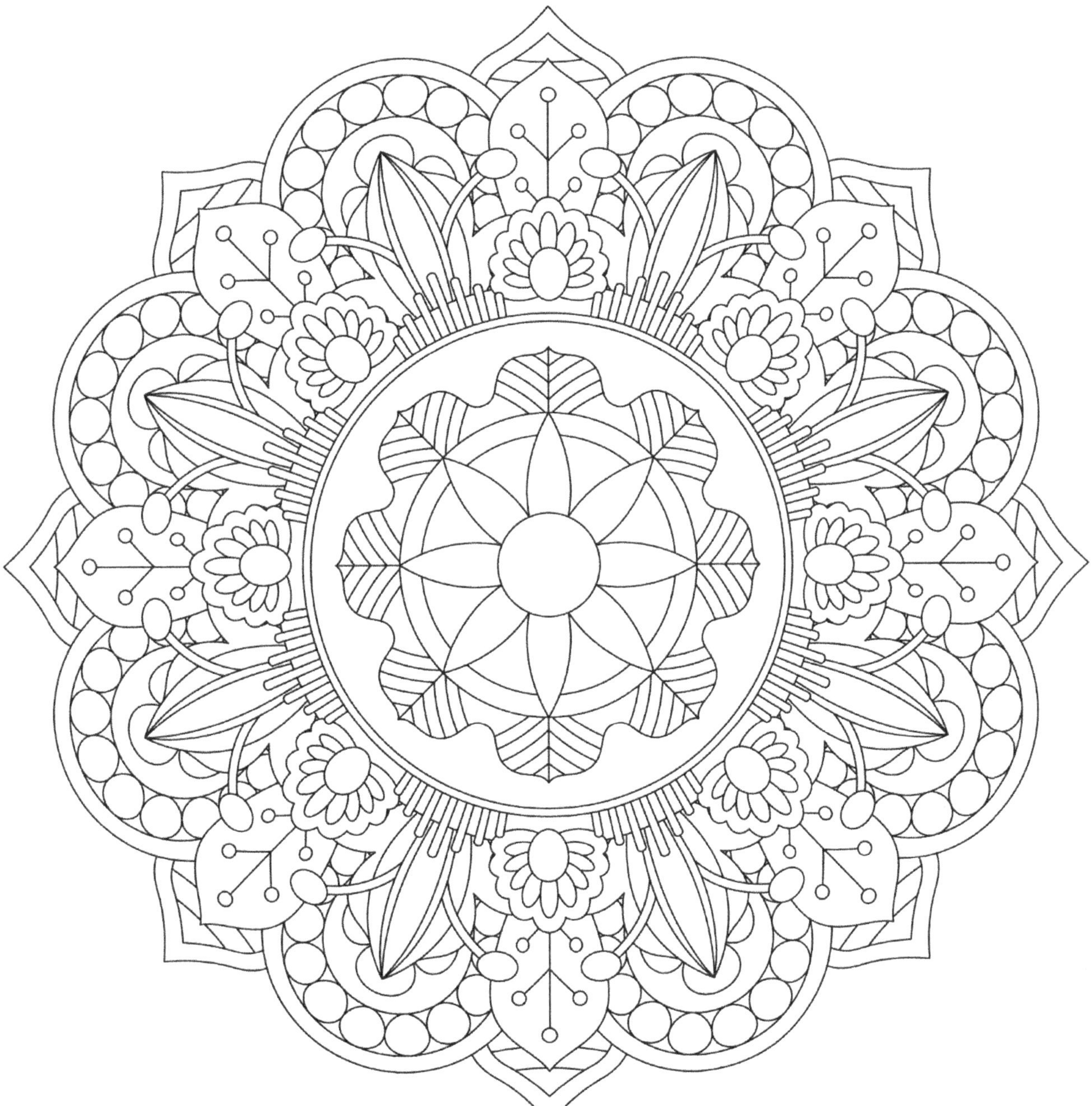

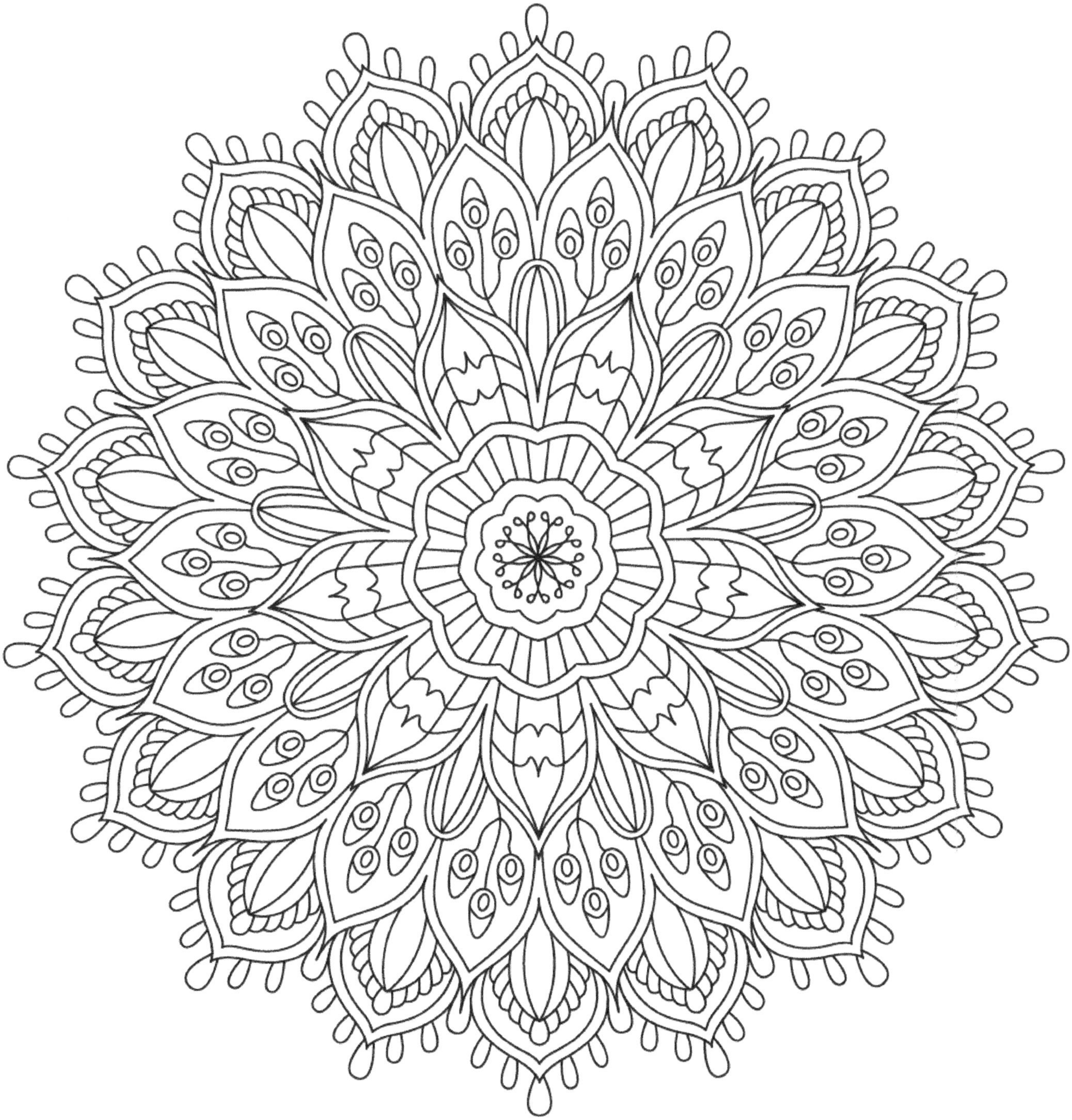

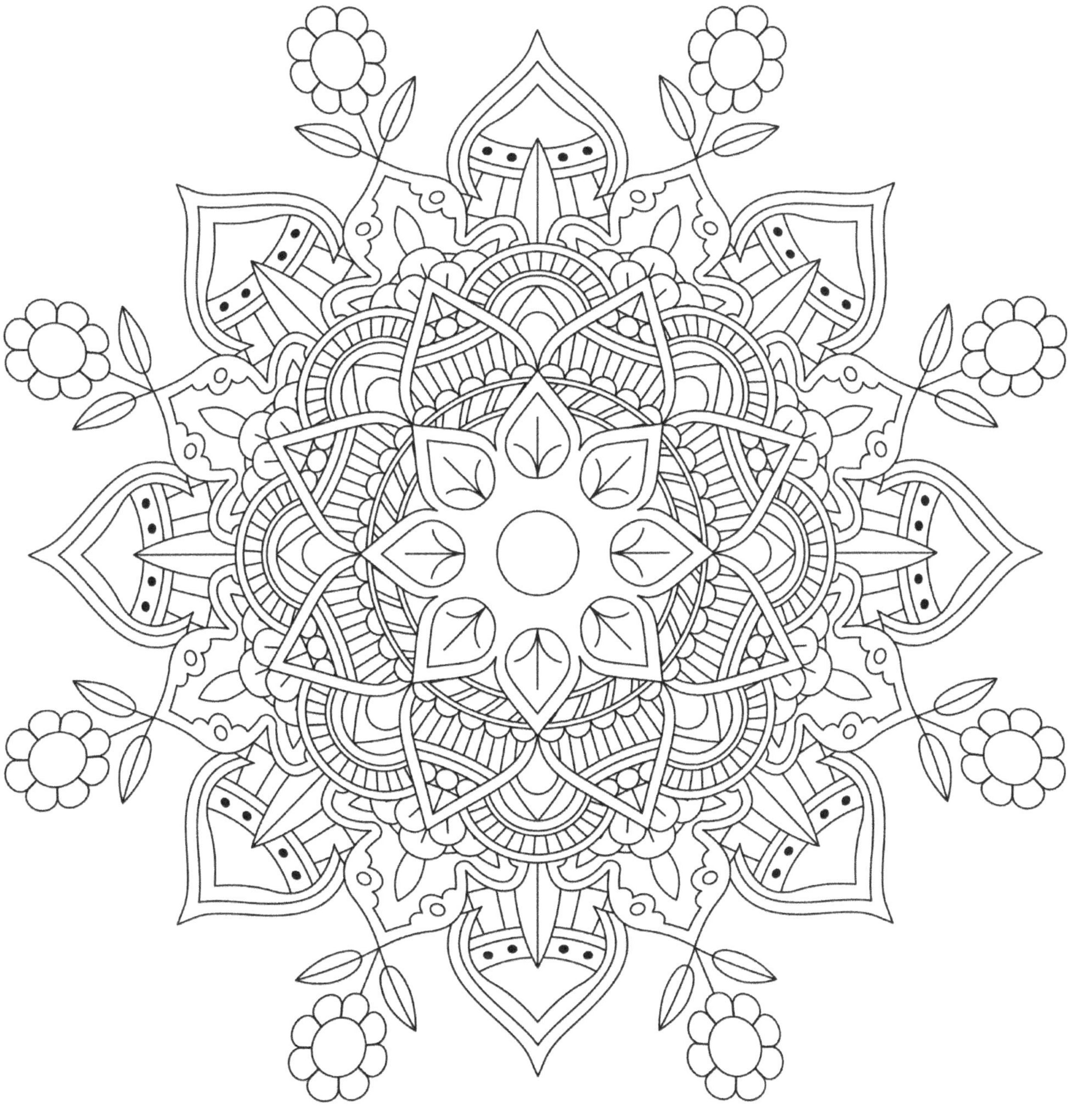

“Take time to do what makes your soul happy”

Made in the USA
Columbia, SC
21 August 2020

17285706R00057